Advance Praise for
The Choreography of Customer Service

"A detailed and doable playbook for delighting customers where it counts…in the real world. Highly recommended!"

—Jay Baer, co-author of *Talk Triggers: The Complete Guide to Creating Customers with Word of Mouth*

"The best business leaders understand that brands which stand the test of time are all ultimately focused on one thing: people. This book is a must read for anyone wanting to unlock the secrets of more meaningful customer interactions, growth, and lasting success."

—Brent Gleeson, bestselling author of *Taking Point* and *Embrace the Suck*

"Chris has a spirit of excellence in all he does. As the sages of our industry have passed the torch, I am personally proud to be a witness to his continued truth and integrity in action."

—Claudia Marshall author, trainer, franchisee, and former International Training Director for Arthur Murray

THE CHOREOGRAPHY OF CUSTOMER SERVICE

High Touch Service in a Touch Free World

CHRIS LYNAM

Post Hill
PRESS

A POST HILL PRESS BOOK
ISBN: 978-1-63758-216-9
ISBN (eBook): 978-1-63758-217-6

The Choreography of Customer Service:
High Touch Service in a Touch Free World
© 2022 by Chris Lynam
All Rights Reserved

Cover Design by Matthew Revert

Post Hill Press
New York • Nashville
posthillpress.com

Published in the United States of America
1 2 3 4 5 6 7 8 9 10

Mom, you taught me that running a business and
a family was possible and I am so grateful.

Dad, you taught me that storytelling can make
more connections than hard facts ever will.

To Christian, Olivia, Violet, Evelyn, and Ava Rose -You
are five miraculous treasures in my life's quest.

To Daisey, my everything partner. This book would still be an idea
I would have talked about writing someday if it weren't for you.
You have the unique ability to transform a someday into a today.

CONTENTS

Foreword ix

Preface... xi

Introduction.. xv

Chapter 1 The Secret Mission 1

Chapter 2 The Backstory....................................... 19

Chapter 3 The Negative....................................... 39

Chapter 4 Muscle Memory 49

Chapter 5 Return on Investment............................. 71

Chapter 6 Let the Choreography Begin.................... 87

Chapter 7 Adding a Frame 105

Chapter 8 Depth and Altitude 121

Chapter 9 The Way You Make Me Feel.................... 137

Chapter 10 Putting It into Action............................ 153

Epilogue 167

Acknowledgments.. 173

FOREWORD

In my years of speaking and training professionals to be more effective in the workplace, there is a constant: It is a forever battle between sharing what people want versus what they need. There are those who see training as a threat, like someone offering them an endless indefinite walk through a desert. Then there are others who see training as an outstanding opportunity to grow. If you can discover the blend of information, writing style, and storytelling, a breakthrough can occur.

I first met Chris after noticing his posts online about my book, *QBQ! The Question Behind the Question*. When I sent him a note of gratitude, he shared how much *QBQ!* helped his business and offered to write a review of *QBQ!* Minutes later, there was a beautifully written five-star review online that blew my socks off.

Over time, Chris and I kept in touch. When I joined him for an interview on his podcast, I remember thinking he is the kind of person I'd want in the front row of my own speaking engagements. Simply put, Chris is a learner who demonstrates a positive attitude mixed with gratitude as he engages in meaningful conversation.

So, here we are now with a book authored by Chris, the learner. I'm grateful to have played a part in his business, book writing, and personal development. More importantly, his message of Customer Service has never been more essential than it is today. Through critical information, delightful storytelling, and a relatable style of writing, this book can be the tool you're looking for to become even more effective tomorrow than you are today!

So get started right now—and enjoy!

John G. Miller
Author of *QBQ!*
QBQ.com
Denver, Colorado USA

PREFACE

I was paralyzed. My hands were frozen to the steering wheel, and the exhaust of my old Mustang was the only reminder to my brain that I wasn't completely catatonic. I wanted desperately to get out, but I couldn't. Had there been smartphones in 1999 or dashboard cameras in 1968 Mustangs, they would have seen me in the driver's seat, my body language as if I were being held at gunpoint by someone hiding in the back. But there was no gun, and there was no one else in the car—I was being held captive by my nerves.

From the outside, you would have just seen an old Mustang with the headlights off and the engine running, but inside was a guy who desperately wanted to start a new life and find an identity—and was already five minutes late for an interview that was only ten feet away.

What I wanted, to interview for a job as a dance teacher, was stifled by what I wasn't willing to do: get out of my car.

So, with every fiber of my heart screaming for me to snap out of it, to walk in, face my fear, and interview for the job, I made up my mind: I decided to drive home. My nervous brain went to work trying to soothe my poor choice with its own version of pop-up banner ads for me to click on to rationalize my stupidity. *They probably didn't really want you to interview tonight anyway*, one would say, or *it was probably just a scam, you saved yourself the trouble.* Each one of these thoughts was part of a greatest-hits playlist I had collected over the years to rationalize my poor effort, performance, or decision-making. If there was a recipe for regret, then I was a master chef.

The regret stung for a while, but eventually, retreating from that interview was something that shifted further into the back of my mind, like a new best friend you meet at a week-long summer camp that you'll never see again. In a way, this story is no different from so many customers in any industry in the world.

At some point, the customers you've seen (or never met) have reached the perimeter of their comfort zone—alone. Maybe they aren't sitting in an old Mustang, but they certainly let old behavior override a new adventure—no matter how wonderful and life-changing that adventure may be.

Think of how much our civilization has changed in a field like medicine. The brainpower, technology, and research dedicated to extending or saving someone's life is dramatically different from generation to generation. But when it comes to saving the lifespan of a customer, too many businesses are experiencing too many losses.

In the case of my job interview, I got home, slapped myself in the face, screamed in the mirror, and scraped together the courage to show up the following day for an interview I was now a day late for. In the case of our customers, we don't often get a second chance like that.

In a business landscape that has gone through drastic changes around the world, we can't afford to rely on second chances. We can't allow our customer-saving tools to be dirty or our ability to diagnose communication breakdowns to be numb. A Civil War doctor could still be called a doctor regardless of their mortality rate, just like a customer service representative can still be called a professional regardless of the service they provide.

That can change when we invest our brainpower, technology, and research into customer service. This can be your start. The beginning of a mission to acquire the skills to save a single customer that would have otherwise abandoned their shopping cart, discontinued using your product, or chosen to retreat to their comfort zone.

Every day of my job at Arthur Murray Dance Studio is a reminder of how close I came to missing this path of my life entirely. Hopefully, someone will look at your business, the service they received, and the joy your product brought to them with the same gratitude.

INTRODUCTION

There's a magical phrase that can turn grown men into grumpy walking hat stands: "I just want to go try a few things on." I heard this phrase many years ago, on the night of our anniversary, when my wife, Daisey, dragged me along to shop for a new outfit. When we got to the store, she hung all of her earthly belongings on my limbs and bolted off through clothing-store Disneyland. Having done this many times before, I knew the drill. I found a comfy spot outside the fitting room and, as per the terms and services agreement outlined in my marriage, I proceeded to give feedback on her outfits as she modeled them.

This wasn't a new activity, but it was a new store. Since this was in the ancient times before the iPhone, I'm sure I looked bored out of my mind as I waited for her. Then, a question changed everything: "Hey man, do you want a beer or something while you wait?"

It took me by surprise. Here was a store employee that I hadn't seen when we walked in, and he suddenly appears offering me a beer? Maybe this was a euphemism of some sort or a trick wives play on their husbands to see just how disinterested they are in shopping for clothes. Whatever it was, it sounded too good to be true. All of those thoughts were articulated when I responded to the store employee with confusion. But he just smiled and said, "You look like you could use a beer. We've got Heineken in the back. Is that okay?"

Heineken? That was my beer of choice. "Sure!" I blurted out. When he handed me the beer, I was no longer a grumpy walking hat stand; I was just a guy, reclining in a chair, holding a Heineken while his wife shopped. Not bad. It was ice cold, and maybe it was the circumstances, but it was the best Heineken I've ever had.

Based on the clothing, Daisey was falling in love with the store; based on the beer, I couldn't blame her. I was enjoying myself. My beer angel came by to check in on me. He offered me another beer and mentioned, casually, "You know, with your tall and lean build, our menswear would fit you really well." When you have the long arms of a basketball player, finding dress shirts that fit, and look good, is about as easy as Indiana Jones finding the Ark of the Covenant—not easy at all. He continued, "What are you, a thirty-six/thirty-seven sleeve?" And he was spot on. As I answered in the affirmative, I was stunned yet impressed. "Then this is going to be your new favorite store." And it was. Shopping at that store became a regular tradition for us for almost a decade afterward. As great as the clothes were, and they sure did fit great, it was the customer service we kept going back for.

Now, I look back on that beer moment, and I can appreciate it not just as the consumer but also as someone who has been training customer service professionals for over two decades.

I work in the ballroom dance industry where our service desk is the space between our elbows (we literally hold our clients in our arms) and faking the connection we create is impossible. It's close-range, high-touch service, and it takes a lot of hard work to make what we do look easy.

In the case of my beer guy, he was smooth, the conversation was natural, and his service skills were most certainly the byproduct of great training. He made it look easy, which is what great customer service should be like; he could definitely have worked in our industry, without question. His company's investment in the beer, and their training program, definitely paid off.

■ ■ ■

Unfortunately, for every story like this, there are countless interactions where the service is forced, impersonal, or nonexistent. The type of service that makes you want to put the word *service* in air quotes. The kind that makes you wonder where the manager is, what the hiring standards are, or what the culture of the organization is as a whole. Studies show that bad customer service is responsible for over $60 billion in lost revenue, and that number is increasing every year. In another study, over 80 percent of participating company executives stated that customer service was their number one priority. You don't have to be a customer service conspiracy theorist to see the irony here.

For years, great service was a way to differentiate a business from its competition. Today, with competition coming from all over the world and a pandemic changing the business landscape as we know it, customer service skills might be the difference between a business keeping their doors open and one closing for good.

The bottom line is this: customer service has never been more important than it is today.

As a business owner, I felt like every book I read on sales, communication, leadership, and human behavior was extending my education so I could better equip my staff. So, I wanted to write the kind of book that I would love to find and read on a work trip, use as a catalyst for staff training, and/or create a competitive advantage for my business.

As a father of five, and someone who loves to read to his kids, I know how quickly attention spans can shift. So, each chapter of this book includes a story to keep you engaged and entertained, and to help drive home a clear example of the teaching.

As a teacher, I know that information is only as valuable as the application you put behind it. Some of the best advice I ever received in my career came from my old boss, Bobby Gonzalez, who said, "If you want to be great at this job, you just need two things: good health and an open mind." This book could be the catalyst that improves your business, or it could be a waste of space on your bookshelf. Good health and an open mind will determine how you see and use it.

The late Zig Ziglar sold cookware before he became a famous author and speaker. John Maxwell was a preacher before he became an expert on leadership. While their industries may be different from yours, there is one common denominator: people. I'll tell you right away that this book includes some stories about dancing, but at the heart of it all, according to author Brené Brown, is "just people, people, people."

This book takes you through three stages:

1. The Choreography: I'll introduce the primary concepts of high-touch service. We'll cover our Customer Service Components—the building blocks of our choreography. This will apply to any product or service and equip you and your team beyond the *dos* and *don'ts* of a basic training manual.
2. The Connection: You'll learn how to add more depth to your service choreography, take the guesswork out of how to create a great experience, and make a more lasting impression with your clients.
3. The Commitment: We'll explore how the choreography works when there are objections, misunderstandings, and other pressurized situations.

Every great monument, bridge, or building began with a bold idea, a builder willing to take on the challenge, and a blueprint. Whether it's the Wright brothers or Elon Musk, history is filled with stories where the skeptics far outnumbered the visionaries. In the world of dance instruction, we know a lot about skeptics. Our product is something that people love the idea of but are convinced they're incapable of doing. We deal with fears and phobias that have become affixed to people's identities, only to see that all wash away when they allow us to teach them.

Fixing customer service is no different. The divide between the service we deliver and the service we want might be wide—so wide that people believe that reaching the other side is a fool's errand. Who's to say that you can't be the visionary, the engineer that constructs the bridge that can change your skills, your career, and your industry? This is your blueprint, and I'm so grateful to have a chance to explore it with you.

CHAPTER 1

The Secret Mission

The doorbell chimed. It was dark enough, and rainy enough, to make anyone wonder: *Who would be here at a time like this?* I flipped on the porch light, and in front of me was a young boy, about ten years old, drenched and holding a bucket. My heart went out to him immediately. "Hey, can I help you?" Instead of responding, he reached into his pocket and produced a laminated card.

"Hello," he read from the card, which looked older than he was, "my name is Joey, and I'm raising money to improve the lives of disadvantaged youth in our city." Then, like a pirate revealing his treasure, he lifted the lid on his bucket. As someone who had sold everything from chocolate bars to cookbooks for school fundraisers in grade school, I was hoping the bucket would contain more of the former, and not the latter. I heaved a sigh of relief to see an assortment of candy and chocolate bars, but then one thing caught my eye, and I tuned everything else out: Red Vines, my movie-watching treat of choice—I could eat them by the tub. At that point, I was Joey's captive audience. The only problem? I was Joey's captive audience.

Joey continued his presentation, and I was stuck. I tried smiling, nodding, giving every sign that I was on his side and ready to purchase. But he kept reading, as steady as the rain pouring down behind him; he was determined to read every last word on his script. My eyes darted from the licorice, to Joey, to the script, and as he continued to share all of the specific details of his cause, my heart went out to him. How many people would wait this long to buy some candy? I realized that every line of Joey's script must have felt like a recipe to him. And once he assembled all the ingredients, I would buy on the spot. But all I was thinking was, *Get to the pitch. Just ask me if I want to buy some candy.* My hopes began to rise as he set his script down, but they were dashed immediately as he started to describe the inventory of his candy tub. At this, I stopped him and asked, "Hey, buddy, how much for the Red Vines?"

"Five dollars," he said. My internal price point was far, far lower, but my affinity for the licorice, and the fact that I'd endured the entire presentation, prompted me to take some corrective action.

I grabbed a pen and a small notebook and handed them to Joey. Right there, on the porch on a rainy winter's night, I gave a ten-year-old kid a lesson on how to improve his presentation. I assured him that I'd be purchasing something if he could deliver this new and improved pitch. We edited down the presentation to the bare essentials. Since I knew he could read from a script, this new, leaner version would be a breeze in comparison. At first, he eyed me as if expecting a prank. But I kept assuring him, kept teaching him, and he diligently wrote everything down. "Now I'm going to close the door again," I said, "You knock, I'll answer, and then you give your new presentation." He knocked on the door and began.

"Hi, I'm Joey, and I know it's late," he said. I nodded my approval, and he opened up the bucket: "But maybe this will help. I could read you this long message," he held up his script, "or I could just tell you that everything I sell in this bucket will help me go to college. So, can you help me with that?"

After he'd recited the new and improved pitch, I bought all the Red Vines he had.

■ ■ ■

Whether or not you're selling candy door-to-door, there's something about Joey's story that anyone in customer service can benefit from: a new point of view. Like so many others, he was doing everything that was asked of him: visiting houses, reading his script, opening his candy bucket, and hoping that added up to more candy sold. When people said no, I'm sure he was trained to accept the rejection, wave goodbye, and move on. But where's the improvement in all of that?

I taught Joey something I call The Secret Mission, and it's exactly what you're going to learn next. It's also important to note that, though this book is about customer service, service without sales is like a movie without Red Vines, at least for me anyway. Whether it's being of service or delivering a service, service and sales are symbiotic partners.

The Secret Mission is the best place to start in our journey through Service Choreography because it's how everyone I've trained learns to present ideas with confidence, to clarify a better path to the product, to create more value in the process, and to take ownership in the idea, even if they aren't owners of the company.

THE SECRET MISSION: WHAT IT IS AND WHY IT MATTERS

Mr. and Mrs. Simmons canceled more dance lessons than they took in my one year of teaching them. It was incredible. Each time they'd arrive, I'd be surprised that they'd actually shown up, and they'd be surprised that they had forgotten everything I had taught them. It was as if we were replaying their first lesson, step by step, once a month. Each time I'd schedule their lesson, something would inevitably get in the way, and by their ninth lesson, they were blaming me for their lack of progress. When I look back on their lessons, they might have been right.

The Secret Mission is the point in customer service where you can see a flaw in the status quo and present an alternative that will lead to a better experience. I never did that with Mr. and Mrs. Simmons, not once. I taught their lessons. I was polite, professional, and even smiled while they questioned my ability to teach them, but I never changed my delivery. I gave them the service they expected but didn't deliver the right service.

Knowing what I know now, and how it turned out for them, I would have mustered up the courage to challenge their strategy instead of being the victim of it. I would have let them know that they had exactly the right dance program but entirely the wrong schedule. I would have been the leader they needed instead of the follower they've now forgotten like so many dance steps.

If I had the courage to say that, to stand in the face of the status quo and deliver my Secret Mission, then Mr. and Mrs. Simmons would have had the opportunity to share a lifetime of dance moments together. Even if they declined the option, I would have had the satisfaction in knowing that I gave them the option. Instead, I'm left with regret for what could have been, and they've probably long forgotten about the year they took dance lessons.

Every company, in every industry, will have some version of this story, the one that got away. Not only is it prevalent, but it's also bound to repeat itself. Leadership expert John Maxwell said in his book *No Limits: Blow the Cap Off Your Capacity*, "**Everything worthwhile** in life—everything you want, everything you desire to achieve, everything you want to receive—**is uphill**. The problem is that most of us have uphill dreams but downhill habits. And that's why we have a cap on our production capacity."

Fair warning: The Secret Mission is a choice to go uphill, to challenge the gravitational pull of what's easy with our customers, and to deliver a message that could be the difference between a forgotten experience and a lasting one.

THE THREE SECRET MISSION TYPES

Now it's time for us to take this concept and turn it into something that you can use with your next client. There are three Secret Mission types to give you some variety in your Service Choreography and some ideas below on where and how to apply each one.

1. The Opportunity: How to turn an ordinary option into an enticing opportunity. "Not many people know about this route, but it will save you an hour each way if you take it."
2. The Challenge: When low expectations are met head on with a vision of optimism, you have The Challenge. "Everyone out there doesn't think you have what it takes to win, here's how we're going to shut them all up."
3. The Forecast: A bold prediction of what will take place if they follow your plan. "And then, when you receive that award, just know, I'll be celebrating the journey you've gone through to get it."

What type of response to your plan do you foresee? Think of the desired reactions to a surprise party, home show makeover, or wedding dress reveal. "This is going to bring them to tears!"

Secret Mission: The Opportunity

The Secret Menu

"No one knows that the best dessert we serve isn't really even on the menu," the waiter said (with the confident grin of an infomercial host) to a pair of women in business attire seated a few feet away from me. It was Friday, and I was picking up "date night to go" from our favorite steak house, a fancy meal we'd eat after the kids went to bed. As soon as I overheard him, I became a professional eavesdropper. I needed to know what this dessert was. His audience took the cue and leaned in like a huddle of high school students sharing lunch and juicy gossip. I watched as he flipped over the menu and began the restaurant equivalent of a magic show. He pointed to the menu and began to describe the side dishes. In my mind, I took an inventory of them: au gratin potatoes, Brussels sprouts, creamed spinach. *What strange dessert magic was this guy suggesting?* I couldn't see how any of them could have qualified as a dessert. But he continued, "We take our sweet potato casserole, hot out of the oven" he said, and then, with a little sleight of hand, deftly flipped to the back of the menu and pointed, "and then, we add a scoop of vanilla ice cream on top. Hands down, it's our best dessert." There were plenty of guttural responses of approval, my own included.

It wasn't just the mystery of it all, or my insatiable love for sweet potato casserole—it was the departure from the norm and the confidence of his delivery. He was a Secret Mission artist. He presented the status quo (the menu), presented an exclusive option (the secret dessert), and shared it all in a fun conversational manner, like a secret among friends. This guy was a real pro. Whether he knew it or not, he was creating an experience out of something that could easily be forgotten. Case in point: This secret dessert scene happened years ago, and I still can't stop thinking about it. I'm not sure I can say that about many other menu items I've encountered in my life. That's the power of presenting your product as an Opportunity.

Applying the Choreography: "Would you like to sign up for our loyalty program?"

Loyalty programs have become a regular part of the retail industry, providing valuable customer data and offering special rewards in exchange.

The Problem?

Shoppers have adapted. Like the infomercials of the 1990s and the pop-up ads of the early 2000s, the loyalty programs so prevalent since 2010 have begun to decline. In a study of more than thirty-four thousand consumers, two-thirds said they'd leave one company and switch to another that provided a better customer experience.

Translation: People might show up for a deal, but they stay for the way you make them feel.

The Solution

The approach we've come to expect (and ignore) is the question, "Would you like to sign up for our loyalty program?" It's standard, straightforward, and predictable. But what if you could make this more conversational, like sharing some fun news between friends? A Nielsen study shows that 84 percent of consumers trust word-of-mouth recommendations. So, let's make this a little less transactional and a little more friendly. Here's how:

1. Try a Statement
   "You might already have one of these already, but another customer I helped saved about three thousand dollars since he started using our loyalty card."

   At this point, just like the secret dessert waiter, it's important to pay attention to the body language of your client or customer.

2. Tune in to Signals
   If they raise their eyebrows, tilt their head toward you, smile, or lean in closer, those are great signs of interest. If they ask a question in response, even better.

3. Ask a Follow-Up Question
   Now is the time to ask a question that keeps you in friendly conversation mode. Here are a few examples:

   "So, what do you think?"

"Want to give it a try?"

"Should we go for it?"

You might ask any of these questions while deciding on a movie with friends, getting adventurous with your sushi order on a date, or planning a vacation. They are conversational, not transactional, and, therefore, friendly. Whether you use these questions or you come up with your own, choose ones that could pass for questions you'd use in conversation with your friends and family.

The Opportunity: Recap

The Opportunity is a Secret Mission that acknowledges the status quo and pivots to an enticing idea. Using a statement instead of a question can give you a chance to share the virtues of the idea and examine their reaction instead of asking an expected question and receiving a dismissive response. In general, sharing The Opportunity helps you, the professional, break free of the standard script that many consumers have already adapted to and avoid.

Secret Mission: Challenging Expectations

Our next version of The Secret Mission occurs when outside expectations are low, challenges are great, and confident plans are necessary. The famous philosopher and pilot, Han Solo, once said, "Never tell me the odds," but in this case, I believe the contrary. Sharing the odds, noting how the chips are stacked against success, can be just the right ingredient to inspire your client to rally alongside you as you share your plan. Here's my favorite example of how that works.

Coach Lopez

"We lost four of our best players to the varsity team. No one thinks you guys have what it takes to win." Robert Lopez's voice echoed throughout the breathless gymnasium. On the outside, this was a team with low expectations, but not to Coach Lopez. "So," he finished, "we are going to outwork everyone." As a member of his team, I can tell you that, when he said "everyone," he wasn't just referring to the other junior varsity teams in our league—he meant everyone, anywhere. Or at least it felt that way.

Basketball players are used to running in practice, and the game itself is full of nonstop action, but we were not even remotely prepared for what Coach Lopez had in store for us. We'd run on the track around the football field, up and down the bleachers, around the entire school, and then return for more instructions. On some days, we'd ascend and descend the bleachers hopping on one leg; other days, we'd sprint twenty-, forty-, and one-hundred-yard dashes, and, if at any point one of us wasn't putting in the effort, we all ran the entire campus as a penalty. And, I should mention, all of this was just the warm-up for our real practice. We'd head inside for a barrage of drills and plays. Lopez pounded them into our muscle memory like a blacksmith; he forged us from disparate pieces of scrap metal into a basketball broadsword.

Coach Lopez had the fiery intensity of a drill sergeant, with precision-level expectations to match. We were his soldiers preparing for combat, and the mission was drilled into us: we've lost our four best guys and the expectations are low, so we're going to outwork everyone and shock anyone who doubted us. Lopez's actual words were a little more R-rated, but you get my drift.

Leaders often wait until things go wrong to begin coaching, focusing on corrective behavior only as soon as it's required. A great leader will catch their team doing something right just as often as they catch them doing something wrong. This was Coach Lopez. His constant reminder of what was at stake—the outside belief combined with our inside solution—occurred whether we were doing well or struggling in practice. The big picture was never withheld.

What resulted was the best team I've ever played on with the best coach I've ever played for. Our team accomplished the mission he'd set out for us; we proved everyone wrong. In the process, we finished the season undefeated and garnered enough attention that our team was featured in the local paper. Fitness expert Fred DeVito once said, "If it doesn't challenge you, it doesn't change you." Based on the challenges we faced, our change was dramatic. So much that there hasn't been a challenge I've faced where my mind doesn't think back to this experience as the high-water mark of both physical difficulty and team transformation.

Applying the Choreography: Creating Positive Change through Challenge

We all want to help create positive change in our clients, regardless of our job title. You don't have to be a basketball coach, or a battlefield commander, to utilize this Service Choreography. Let's take a look at the following Challenging Expectations formula:

Outside Expectations + Inside Work = Secret Mission

Let's explore some of the ingredients to motivate your clients, lead your team, and make the most of those moments where the expectations are lower than the result you believe is possible.

Step 1: What Are the Outside Expectations?

Are you up against a deadline that others believe to be impossible? Is your client facing criticism for the results they desire from your product or service? Whether it's real or imagined, physical or psychological, you must share the outside expectations.

10

Step 2: What Is the Inside Work?

The Inside Work is your leverage. It is your competitive advantage that you will reveal to create differentiation.

Now let's look at some examples of how our Challenging Expectations formula works for different professionals:

Personal Trainers

> The Outside Expectations: "This is the time of year when most people are letting their fitness goals go into hibernation."

> The Inside Work: "But not us. We are going to push harder to reach your goals while everyone else is letting go."

> The Secret Mission: "And, by the time beach season comes around, you're going to be so happy you didn't go into hibernation like everyone else. Are you ready to get started?"

Insurance Brokers

> The Outside Expectations: "So many people wait until there's an earthquake to buy earthquake insurance, only to pay a premium. They wait until they can feel the problem before they find a solution."

> The Inside Work: "But not us. When you run into a problem, the last thing you want is to add to it by not being insured."

> The Secret Mission: "Taking care of this now isn't just about saving money—it's saving you the worry of not being covered when it matters most."

Dance Teachers

The Outside Expectations: "After a big dance event, like a competition or performance, a lot of people exhale, relax, and celebrate by taking some time off from their lessons."

The Inside Work: "But not us. While everyone is relaxing and letting their progress slip, we're going to keep building on the progress you've already made.

The Secret Mission: "This way, by the next competition, we won't be trying to recover old progress; we'll be dancing at a much higher level."

Challenging Expectations: Key Takeaways

A great customer service professional must be a motivator and strategist when there are challenges. They won't let pessimistic opinions or low expectations stop them from formulating a plan and, most importantly, delivering that message. Without barricades, there can be no breakthroughs. Every product, scientific breakthrough, or awesome feat of mankind started with a problem. Whether it was a vaccine or flying to the moon, a corporate turnaround or coaching a basketball team, someone was willing to defy the naysayers, to offer a glimmer of hope where others could only see hopelessness, and to deliver a solution that could change an outlook or even the world.

President Teddy Roosevelt once said, "A soft, easy life is not worth living, if it impairs the fiber of brain and heart and muscle. We must dare to be great; and we must realize that greatness is the fruit of toil and sacrifice and high courage." Your product or service may be wonderful, even life-changing, but that doesn't mean it doesn't have its share of difficulties. This Challenging Expectations approach doesn't hide those inherent challenges, it celebrates them. Roosevelt finishes the quote in true challenge-for-change fashion: "Let us live in the harness, striving mightily; let us rather run the risk of wearing out than rusting out." I think Roosevelt would have loved a guy like Coach Lopez, and I think your customers will appreciate their achievements much more when they know exactly the kind of obstacles you helped them fight through.

Secret Mission: The Forecast

This final version of The Secret Mission is only for the bold. To wield its awesome power, you must have an unwavering belief in your product, service, or idea and a vision for the outcome your client will achieve if they follow your advice. Keep in mind that this isn't clairvoyance; your Forecast is rooted in your experience and professional recommendations. While forecasting is commonplace in meteorology, the stock market, and any company with a sales quota, the practice can be incredibly effective in other, less obvious, applications (like church fishing trips).

Proper Dosing for the Church Fishing Trip

What could go wrong when you mix deep sea fishing, a church congregation, and over-the-counter medication? I was a certified preteen, and my mom had enlisted a friend of the family to take me to the father-son church deep sea fishing trip. Chuck already had kids—two girls—so I was his rental son, and he was my rental dad. We were meeting the rest of the group at the docks just after sunrise, so I spent the night at his house.

I was curled up in my sleeping bag willing myself to sleep. The combination of being in someone else's house, the excitement of the fishing trip, and the fact that I was attempting to sleep before nine o'clock made this a challenge. Just as I was finally drifting off to sleep, Chuck came into the room. I had this paranoid feeling that it was already time to leave for the trip and, somehow, it only felt like I had slept for a few minutes. Chuck reached out his hand and said, "Here, take this." Inside was a small pill and a glass of water and a Secret Mission for the ages. "Everyone takes Dramamine right before they get on the boat, but not us," he said. Even in my bleary-eyed state, this got my attention. "The real trick is to get it in your system the night before, then take it again before you get on the boat." We both took the pill, and as I folded back into my sleeping bag, more grateful for the extra sleep than anything, he said, "Just watch tomorrow and you'll see."

When we arrived at the dock, we greeted the rest of the group. The fathers and their sons made comments about catching dinner, playful bets on who would catch the most fish—and then something peculiar happened. Just before they stepped foot on the boat, I watched them all pop their Dramamine pill. It was like communion, but for motion sickness. Chuck looked over at me and nodded with eyes that said, *You see what I mean?* And I certainly did. Chuck wasn't just my rental dad; he was a bona fide teller of the future.

As part of our plan, Chuck and I both took our second motion sickness pill as we boarded. I was very interested to see how well our plan would turn out. As we set off through the chilly air and choppy waters, I'd find out exactly the kind of expert my rental dad really was.

I'll spare you the explicit details, but let's just say that he was right about it all. Every single member of the church fishing party, except the two of us, were, in his words, "feeding the fish." Each time it happened, it elevated Chuck's expertise, his forecast, and my respect for him, which is a little weird to say, considering my evaluation metrics.

Fine-Tuning Your Forecast

Chuck's suggestion didn't just save me from motion sickness that day, it taught me how to make confident recommendations as a customer service professional. In this section, we'll define the details of Chuck's Forecast so you can fine-tune one of your own.

1. **Every Forecast acknowledges a typical problem.** Chuck had obviously been fishing before and had most likely experienced the problems associated with taking the right motion sickness pills. That experience became the platform for his Forecast.

Your version will be inspired by the problems your clients face. Whether that's the frustration of how to dress for a summer wedding or how to recover from a marketing mishap, remember that great service and problem-solving go hand in hand. And speaking of solutions, let's check out number two.

2. **Every Forecast offers a solution.** Chuck's solution was to get the Dramamine into our systems the night before and to take it again on the dock. It would have been a little dark if Chuck had shared the problem without offering his solution. In your case, the solution is what separates you from the amateurs and elevates you as a professional. Any amateur can find a problem, but professionals can find the solution. (Chuck may not have been a professional fisherman, but he certainly gave professional advice.)

3. **Every Forecast has a comparison.** This is your "not us" moment. When you compare the mistake that most people make to the option that you're proposing, it gives it clarity and context. "Most people sign up for the basic level only to run into problems integrating with their other business apps. But not us. By going immediately to the premium package, we eliminate all of your future integration headaches."

4. **Every Forecast makes a clear prediction backed by evidence.** Sharing a confident expectation of what will happen to those who do take your advice, and those who don't, is the final stage of the Forecast. There should be evidence to support that the customer is on the right track, like the landmarks they may see if you had given them driving directions. The more detail you provide, the clearer the process becomes.

Finding Your Forecast

Let's take a look at how The Forecast could work in different industries. Keep in mind that the wording and use of the four points above can always be adjusted and rearranged to suit your style.

Realtor

"There are so many people that want a home but never take the steps you did to make that a reality. I want to congratulate you, and when we've wrapped up your paperwork and you're having your first meal in your dining room, I want you to toast to a plan that was years in the making. Thank you for letting me be a small part of that."

Wedding Dance Teacher

"There are so many couples that will spend their time, money, and energy on hors d'oeuvres that everyone will forget and end up with a makeshift first dance because of it. Not us! I'm so happy that you've taken the time to learn how to dance the right way, the first time. When you take that final bow in front of your loved ones, just know that you will have created a memory that they'll never forget."

It takes courage to create change. It's far easier to accept circumstances, wave the white flag, and hide behind a quote like "the customer is always right," bending its context to fit the perimeter of your comfort zone. Instead, let's think of another quote, one that is better suited to the change agent you are becoming and not fraught with future regret. "Do not go gentle into that good night. Rage, rage against the dying of the light." Dylan Thomas's words are the perfect summary for The Secret Mission. Until you challenge the status quo, create an enticing plan to add value to your product, and forecast a positive outcome, your customers will leave and go gentle into the good night, never to return.

A study showed that, nine times out of ten, dissatisfied customers stopped doing business with a company without any complaint—they went gently into the night.

The Secret Mission is a challenge that is built for positive change, shared by confident service-minded professionals. Keep in mind that at the root of it all is an unwavering belief in the value of your product and the plan you have to deliver it.

I was once challenged by a business mentor to talk to my students as if they could read my mind. That meant that I definitely couldn't ask them to do something just to improve my paycheck. (*I really want to buy a new suit, so why don't you buy this new program?* No way.) As I began to think more about the advice, I realized that, if I were too conservative with my planning, I wouldn't want that mental soundtrack to come through either. (*I'm not going to ask you to join the event because I'm pretty sure you're not going to do it.*)

After taking a lot of time to think it through, this advice seeped into the core of my communication skills. I decided that the best approach would be to have an exciting plan for all of my students, regardless of their circumstances. There would be challenges to overcome, of course, but I figured that hearing about a plan from an excited professional certainly beat the alternative.

With the mind-reading advice enabled, I began to create Secret Missions for my students. I wrapped my mind firmly around the benefits they'd receive by stretching past the confines of their comfort zone. I'd focus intently on the value of participating in events they'd never tried, and even if they didn't say yes, they were grateful for the opportunity.

Bottom line: You can share your confident plan with your customer or stay quiet and wait for them to agree to your competitor's confident plan. Think of what they have to gain, the value they'll get, and the benefits they'll experience, then share it with them. Go further and forecast the future if they follow the plan. The Secret Mission is your chance to rage against the dying of the light, and your customers will appreciate it.

CHAPTER 2

The Backstory

The punch was like nothing I'd felt before. It was both an attack and a warning. "You don't belong here," it said. I was hurt and confused. The news I shared had the exact opposite response to what I was expecting, like taking a swig from a milk jug to find out (the wrong way) that it had gone bad. This situation had gone bad, and my composure was fading. The news, in this case, was that I was following my heart. My audience was a girl, Scarlet, who I thought cared about me, but her response hit me right in the feelings.

But sometimes, great stories are found in the wreckage.

We had met while swing dancing. It was the late nineties, swing had gone through a retro revival, and the scene swept me up like a beacon of hope wrapped in vintage clothes. My story could have been one of a depressed athlete, injured and coming to grips with a life without my childhood dream. I didn't have basketball, but I was still tall, and my height was a constant reminder of my former identity. Then swing came along. It was enveloping, from my clothing to my music choices—everything had to be vintage. It was as if I was trying to eliminate any evidence of the current day so I could travel back in time.

Scarlet was a low-key celebrity in the swing dancing scene. She taught at a popular club in San Francisco and had even done some professional swing dance work for music videos. Hearing that you could make money from swing dancing sounded like someone paying you to go to Disneyland. Maybe she took pity on me. We ran into each other after I had been stood up on a date. We danced together, exchanged numbers, and eventually started dating. Deep down, I knew I wasn't at her dance level, so I wanted to do anything possible to get caught up, even if that meant quitting my job. You may not think to quit your job to get better at dancing, but you probably didn't work where I was working—I was looking for any excuse to leave.

I had the kind of job you'd get that paid enough to keep you working full time but crummy enough to make you miss being a full-time student. It was an ice-cold logistics warehouse that supplied Silicon Valley with all of their important marketing material. Out of everyone running, climbing ladders, and driving forklifts to fill our orders, can you guess who was the one lucky guy to have a desk in the middle of it all? That's right, yours truly. I felt like a data entry clerk for some Siberian prison. Can you see now why I was in the market for something better? I was tired of wearing a parka to work and feeling isolated at a desk and wondered if I could find something that allowed me to socialize.

I had seen the ad before, filed under *D* in the newspaper for *dance*, but I dismissed it as a scam. "Dance instructor training program"—it just seemed too good to be true. But then, one day, there were two ads. The one I assumed was a scam was still there, but the new one was for Arthur Murray Dance Studio.

Arthur Murray was a name I had heard of. There was the song "Arthur Murray Taught Me Dancing in a Hurry," and I knew that it was a brand name when it came to dancing. (I wouldn't find out until later that it was a worldwide company with the longest history in teaching ballroom dancing.) So, I figured, if one dance employment ad was fake,

I had a well-known backup plan. Why would a brand name like Arthur Murray run an ad that was a scam? And maybe, just maybe, this was my ticket out of the freezer and up to Scarlet's dance level. I had to tell her.

I decided to skip work and spend the day with her. It was one of those typical San Francisco winter days that would feel like spring any place else. Maybe it was the weather, or the news I was keeping, but if you picture the moment in a musical just before the actor breaks into a song, that's what this day was like. Only it wasn't.

"Hey, so, I'm thinking about getting a job at Arthur Murray," I said. She looked at me with an expression I couldn't quite make out. If she was excited, she was covering it up really well.

"As what?" She asked. It wasn't really a question at all. She stated it, and it stung.

I shot back, and my voice faltered. "As the freaking janitor, alright?" I was reeling. "No, as a dance teacher," I said. "They have a training program for new dance teachers."

She said nothing. The quiet was unsettling to say the least. I took a deep breath to compose myself. It wouldn't be enough. Then she said, "You'll never be any good at that."

And that was it, the knockout blow. At least, that's how it felt.

She must have realized what she had done because she started filling in a series of professional-to-amateur words of advice that never got past the filter of my hurt feelings. So I left and made my decision.

Sometimes the gut punch of painful words can be just the push you needed but never asked for. It was the fuel that motivated me to call, set up an interview, and eventually end up getting a job at Arthur Murray Dance Studio, the company I'm still with today. The company responsible for fulfilling my dream of becoming a professional athlete, the place where I discovered a passion for teaching that I never knew I had, and most importantly, the place that led to my greatest lucky break of a lifetime. It's how I met my wife, Daisey.

The day of my interview, the studio manager greeted me with a smile, looked me in the eye, and shared, "You know, a tall guy like you would do great in ballroom competitions." I was sold. What he saw was a tall, college-aged guy with swing dancing experience, holding his resume and determined to get the job.

What he didn't see was my Backstory, the sequence of events that led to me ending up there. The internal and external motivations that were the real reason why I walked through the door.

WHAT IS THE BACKSTORY?

The Backstory is the most powerful part of the Customer Service Choreography because it is the most personal. It is the origin story of how your client crossed paths with your product or service. It comprises the internal and external forces that prompt someone to seek out your business. These can be rational or emotional, open or guarded, but all will require an interested customer service professional to discover.

In film, characters without a Backstory are referred to as flat. They lack depth and may have some momentary function in the story, but they aren't the ones that resonate in your mind when it's over.

Customer Service is no different. Until we take the time to learn about how our customers arrived, what motivated their decisions, or what they overcame to see you, they'll all be flat characters lacking depth. Eventually, they'll become just another nameless and faceless character in your career narrative.

THE MISSION

In dancing, those that lack training and technique are flat. They need a high quantity of flashy moves to gain a little attention. The best dancers are trained from the inside out. They can make even the simplest movements look beautiful and memorable. Let's learn some now.

Our mission together is to enhance your customer service technique, not just supply you with dozens of flashy lines filled with five-dollar words.

YOUR TOOLS

At the heart of The Backstory is being a great interviewer. What your client might arrive with is like a resume, it's the cover story. Your job, as a great interviewer, is to understand the person behind the resume, the real story. That begins with questions that prompt conversation, continues with interest in their responses, and will adjust as necessary to keep the momentum of communication active.

Question Types

Open-ended, or open-probe, questions are designed to stimulate conversation because they can't be answered with a single yes or no response.

Closed-ended, or closed-probe, questions may not prompt longer responses but can help increase the pace of a conversation. Listen to the difference:

> "What was the best part of your lesson today?" versus
> "Did you like your lesson today?"

A great conversationalist will use a mixture of both open- and closed-ended questions. You'll do this without much thought with your loved ones, and with some practice, this can become a consistent skill with your clients.

Conversation Extenders

> "…and then what?"

> "No."

"You're kidding."

Think back to the last conversation where you were hearing some juicy gossip. The kind where you want to draw out every detail with as much description as possible. Did you use any of those responses? Those are conversation extenders. They are designed to encourage the speaker to keep going, to elaborate, to gush. These work wonders in conversation and are a great method for connecting like a friend would.

Your Energy Score

Finally, let's look at one of the most essential tools: your energy score. This is a simple way to address your tone of voice, inflection, and overall engagement in a conversation.

Here's how it works: on a range from one to ten we are going to rate your reactions to certain conversational encounters. Think about how you might look and sound in each situation.

On the low end would be someone boring you. It's to the point that you can barely keep your eyes open and you want to shut the conversation down. Let's call that a one. Can you picture it in your mind? Maybe it's a telemarketer or the stuffy, tweed professor that lulled everyone in class to sleep.

The peak end of our range would be a total release of positive energy. Think of things like summer camp, sporting events, or sharing some major announcement. It's exuberance without apology.

Now that we have the two ends of our energy score, let's find the middle. Think of this as polite conversation that is not negative enough to offend but not positive enough to have resonance. This could be someone in food service, a teacher of some kind, or any other professional, or forgettable, conversation.

Now let's examine how this works. If your client was sharing some news with you about a new promotion at work, that might be a nine. If your response is a two, then they'll feel exposed, that they've overshared, and they will withdraw as a result.

If you sell your product to someone you just met at a ten, but their body language was a one, they will feel overwhelmed, and the nine-point differential will come across as pushy or salesy.

Let's try a quick experiment. See if you can assign as score to each of these players in the scene and you be the judge on what the outcome might be. Ready?

Department store. A customer is eyeing the dress she is holding with a wide smile. While she waits in line, she holds it up to her body, sneaks a peek in the mirror, and does a quiet celebration. When she gets to the front of the line, the floor associate takes a pile of clothes from the counter, walks them back toward the back of the store, returns, and recites, "May I help you?" without any eye contact.

What score would you give the shopper? How about the sales associate? Do you think anyone's score changed from the start of the scene to the end?

Here's how I see it.

The shopper was an eight or nine. The silent celebration and smile were great evidence of someone enthusiastic in an outward way.

The sales associate was a four to begin with. He just seemed a little busy. Leaving or returning without any explanation, apology, or smile is a telltale sign that this person is operating at a substandard level. His score would drop to a one.

Noticing this, our shopper's enthusiasm for the dress wouldn't withstand the lack of enthusiasm from her experience. She'd probably buy the dress but the pull of the sales associate's low score would drag hers down as well. In the words of one of my business mentors, the late Jacques de Beve, "It's not the place, it's the people." We can enhance that further by saying, "It's not the product or the place; it's the people."

Takeaway

We now have a basic understanding of the tools we'll use. This will give us some additional terms we can use as we add to our technique later in the book. Next, we are going to explore where we can use them.

FOUR TYPES OF BACKSTORY

We know The Backstory is designed to help us understand the motivation of our clients. Just like any journey of discovery, there are areas we want to explore further or avoid at all costs.

1. The Backstory You Need: The basic information to do your job
2. The Backstory You Expect: Anticipating the audience to give better service
3. The Backstory You Know: The stage where average agents get stuck
4. The Backstory You Discover: The breakthrough we want to achieve

The Backstory You Need

Some jobs require information from the customer to proceed. This is the Backstory you need. A hairstylist shouldn't start chopping away at your hair until they get some insight from you first. The same can be said for interior designers, all manner of sales jobs, and even your local barista. If they want to deliver a basic level of service, they'll ask you the question, "how would you like it?"

A question like this informs the professional and allows them to deliver the right thing.

These professionals often have more Backstory than they sought out to begin with. Why? Because people want to share their story. The

Backstory is like a secret you're dying to tell someone. Once you've bonded through the essentials, don't be surprised if the Backstory accumulates.

In dancing, we need to find out a timeframe until a big reunion or wedding our students want to dance at. This helps us dole out the right amount of dance information to match their goals.

Dangers of Needed Backstory

Once people begin sharing, they'll usually get comfortable and want to continue. Sadly, there are representatives out there that cut it short. Like an attorney on a courtroom TV show saying "no further questions," they end the connection once they have the information necessary to proceed with their job.

In their defense, these jobs can be tricky to perform, and conversation may be hard to pull off—like dentists, for example—but people are social creatures and wired for connection. Nevertheless, when the potential conversation is stopped short, the client will attempt to keep it going. I like to call this "the haircut question."

This is a term I came up with while training communication skills with our dance instructors. Since we deal with a product that stretches people far outside their comfort zones, we've got to make a great connection to build trust and put our students at ease. To do so, we train our staff to be expert interviewers, focusing the conversation on the student and not ourselves. But if the conversation comes to a lull, it's normal for the client to fill in the dead space. So, as you're reading this, think of the question you might ask a new hairdresser to break a long silence as you're getting your hair done.

"So how long have you been cutting hair?"

For some reason, that's just standard conversational fare in that scenario. I teach our staff that if the students are getting to the dance version of the "haircut question," then we've let the conversation lag.

The Solution

Remember that the information you need is just the starting point, not the finish line. Need-based questions (like "What color are you looking for?" and "What size can I help you find?") should be paired with interest-based questions (like "Where do you see yourself using this?" and "What do you think of their new collection?").

The best example I've experienced is with real estate agents. They use a seamless mix of these questions to help you find the right home and feel like you've done so with the right person. The result is a custom-tailored master class in connection. They use interest-based questions like "What's your vision for this room?" to pair with need-based questions like "How many bedrooms?" While many representatives will get a little gun-shy when talk shifts to finances, a great real estate professional needs that information; however, they will usually ask it in a more connecting manner: "Let's talk price range. What are we looking at?"

They are connection machines. One minute you're meeting them at a property and the next you're telling them how many kids you want to have.

If you find that your clients are filling in long silences with questions directed at you, then try inserting a few more questions to keep the connection going, even if the information isn't vital to you right now. In case you're wondering, my hair guy Mikey not only knows how to cut my hair but also what questions to get the conversation going.

It usually just takes a "So, how's work?" and by the time I finish answering, my haircut is finished.

The Backstory You Expect

We all have a Backstory. In some way, we want to share it with people. Not at the cost of oversharing or breaking societal norms, but what if there was a way to give people a clue? Maybe not as blatant as a sign on your head, but what about a Backstory button on your shirt? That might be just enough for someone to help you find a connection, right?

Disney has them, which should come as no surprise being that their parks are shining examples of great service. Their line of Celebration buttons once began as stickers from the Disneyland cast members and are one of the few free souvenirs for guests in attendance. The buttons are given out to guests celebrating things like first visits to the park, honeymoons, anniversaries, and birthdays. A simple, "Are we celebrating anything today?" question leads to a button. From there, the button acts as a Backstory beacon and cast members can share a nice word or follow up with questions.

The Backstory you expect is anticipating the types of clients you have coming in, even if you've never met them before. In marketing, this is referred to as persona development. In effect, you can create sample versions of prospective visitors to your business. You give them names, address what their needs are, ask what concerns they have, and give them a Backstory. At Arthur Murray, we do this all the time to create realistic training scenarios. This is Ted, he's a busy engineer and has no time to socialize. He has a wedding coming up and doesn't want to embarrass himself on the dance floor.

These buyer personas are so realistic that staff will say, "I just had a Ted come in for a lesson tonight." We see what we are prepared to see, and in Disney's case, even if you can't see it, there's a button that will help.

It makes sense that Disneyland would expect people celebrating special occasions to be there. In fact, it probably doesn't hurt if they treated everyone at the park like they were celebrating a special occasion, even without the button. In our case, learning to dance is a fun activity on the surface, but beneath it is a moment of bravery, a venture outside the norm, and maybe even a life-changing decision—so we treat it like a celebration too.

What to Expect from Here

What's your version of a Backstory Button? Could you stand to benefit from developing some buyer personas? I think so. The sooner that you understand the types of people that frequent your business, the sooner you can begin to look at things through their eyes. Even if their Backstory isn't identical, it will allow you and your team to hit the ground running as Backstory agents, on a mission to connect.

Finally, your product isn't just a product, it's a celebration of some kind. What's the benefit, desired outcome, or purpose behind them using it? Whether it's their very first software upgrade or their tenth year doing business with you, those are Backstory moments we can—and should—certainly expect.

The Backstory You Know

Let's say it's the year 1607, and you're a kid who loves looking at the stars at night. Your version of the known universe is limited to what you can observe and sketch. Your drawings are crude—you have to use a lot of imagination—but the general shape is there as far as you can tell. Then in 1608, something called "Danish perspective glass" becomes all the rage for stargazers young and old. Later, people would refer to it as a telescope, and eventually you have a chance to look through one.

Using it brings the vague forms into clearer shapes, and in that moment, your world changes. As a result, your sketches aren't just inferences but show vivid detail that you have seen. Now, you just want to get closer and to see what else is out there.

Whether it's astronomy, technology, or just looking for your kid's missing shoe in the morning, it would be depressing if we were satisfied with our "known universe." Unfortunately, when it comes to customer service, it's easy to let our search for connection reach a comfortably known place. We develop enough rapport to be friendly, and then we just do the job.

I had a particularly tricky time with this as a new teacher. My mind would be so filled with dance information that I was numb to everything else. I've never bungee jumped before, but I'm pretty sure it would be hard to think about your grocery shopping list while you were waiting. For me, the result was I forgot the names and important facts of my students at a near-criminal level. The dance stuff I wanted to cover muted everything else out.

One embarrassing example of this happened with a couple preparing for their wedding dance. I couldn't tell you their names if I tried, but let's call them Steve and Linda. They were learning the swing but were having a tough time with the footwork. I tried drill after drill to improve their dancing. Steve had a tendency to lean too far back, Linda just wanted to fix it all herself, and I was running out of ideas. So I tried something new. I separated them and decided that would give me the best vantage point for both challenges I was up against.

They both repeated the triple-step, triple-step, rock-step rhythm of the East Coast Swing. I gave Linda some tips on her posture, and then we both turned our attention to Steve, still dancing away, leaning too far back, losing his balance, but gritting it out nonetheless. Even when I offered feedback, he wouldn't stop dancing. Like a marathon runner crushing a cup of water into their mouth, he was a machine.

Linda looked on; her eyes were pleading for him to improve. I danced next to him, demonstrating. "Steve, I think you need to use the balls of your feet more." Steve was in a breathless, swing dancing trance and replied, "Right, more balls, more balls, more balls." What followed was like a time bomb of embarrassment. Slowly, I turned toward Linda to see if she caught what happened. Linda was doing the same. We locked eyes and reached the point of mutual embarrassment where no words are shared. And through it all, Steve was still practicing and repeating "more balls, more balls, more balls."

On the surface, I did my job by delivering the product. They were able to dance together. Steve's mantra never really registered outside of the dance improvement sense. Linda and I never spoke a word of it. We finished our lessons together, said our goodbyes, and I assume they got married and danced together. The only problem was that my job never went beyond the surface. I learned just enough to perform the basic functions of my job and left it at that, which might explain why they left their dance hobby behind.

I never once asked them about their wedding, how they met, or what learning to dance together meant to them. I was stuck in my own known universe, just trying to do the job.

I wish I would have known that doing my job, without connection, was only half right.

The Backstory You Discover

I watched a man at the beach with his wife and son. The wife and son carried shovels. They followed the man everywhere he went. He was holding a metal detector, wearing professional-looking headphones, and a backpack with collapsible arm rests. It was like something out of a spy movie. So while I was playing with my kids, this family of beach treasure hunters would cross in and out of my view. Between the gear and the clear roles each family member played, I could tell this wasn't the first time.

Just as my kids and I were grabbing a snack, it happened. The metal detector man began jumping. Thrusting his hands in the air like his favorite football player had scored a touchdown, his whoops and cheers drowned out from the crashing waves. His index finger and thumb displaying his prize. A ring. I couldn't take my eyes off of the scene. It was the look of someone who could pay some bills that he couldn't have just hours before.

Even though the ring hadn't been something he purchased in the store, he discovered it. Even if he sells the ring, he'll still own the discovery.

When you're working to connect with your clients, you're no different from that man. You're beginning the process with curiosity and belief in the activity. Next, you're listening. You will spend more time listening than anything else. When you have a signal, you're digging.

For us, the ring is when we discover the Backstory of our students—not the immediate needs but the reasons and desired benefits they hope to achieve that might be buried under the surface. Here's an example of one of my favorites.

THE AWAKENING

Everyone with a job has a hire date. Mine was April 1, 1999, but my career didn't really begin until the day a shy student shared her story with me nearly eighteen months later. Shelley had the slumped posture of someone walking in late to an important meeting or across the front row of a movie in progress. Her shoulders were forward, her head was low, and her demeanor seemed to be a constant gesture of apology. Her voice was soft and deferential, and trailing behind her was her little girl, an eight-year-old version of herself. She was so far removed from her comfort zone that even her smile trembled when I greeted her. While teaching her didn't really fulfill the cosmopolitan lifestyle I had imagined as a professional dance teacher, my heart immediately went out to her. I knew the feeling. I wanted to do everything I could to make sure that she didn't regret her decision to walk through the door.

So I tried to make her laugh. I asked her to teach me some Mandarin while I worked as her dance teacher. As you might imagine, Shelley had a tough time making eye contact, but this drew a grin, and she agreed. Then I asked her the question that would change the course of my career forever: "What made you decide to start taking dance lessons?" It took her a minute to reply.

"My husband is a good dancer," she said. I was surprised to hear her say that, and when I asked her if they went dancing together already, she paused for another minute. "No," she said, "but we go to his company Christmas party every year, and there's dancing." She then transitioned into what seemed like a rehearsed speech. "And I just want him to have a good time because he's such a good dancer." The wheels in my head hit a full stop.

"Wait, then who does he dance with?" I asked. She smiled, maintaining her rehearsed demeanor.

"Just some of the ladies from his office," she answered. I was shocked, but she insisted it was okay and that she loved watching him.

Even if she was okay with it, I wasn't. An alarm sounded inside me; I felt like I had absorbed years of her feelings. I felt the hurt, and the polite charade, and the damage it was doing to her. Before I realized what I was saying, I made her a promise: "I'm going to do whatever I can to make sure that you are the only person your husband wants to dance with at his next Christmas party." I needed to say it, even though I wasn't quite sure if it would make any difference. But she smiled, and in that moment, her burden was my burden. In that moment, we became partners.

If there was ever a perfect time in my career deserving of a training montage, it would be with Shelley. We went from a single class per week to two. Two became four and, before long, she was there, with her adorable daughter trailing behind, almost every day of the week. A time-lapse video would show her posture steadily improving with each visit, like a nature video showing a flower from seedling to blossom. Along with that, her shy disposition transformed. She became more confident. Gone were the days of the slumped posture and lowered head; now when she walked into her lessons, she had the look of someone opening the door to a cheerful family gathering. She had become a dancer.

Through the course of our lessons together, she continued to teach me Chinese. I vowed that by the time she had her one-year anniversary as a dance student, I'd teach her entire lesson in Mandarin. So she administered language drills while I administered dance ones. It made for some very memorable lessons. Aside from Mandarin, I also learned that her husband was a black belt in karate and worked half the year overseas, leaving her with both of their kids as a full-time mom. He had been with the company for seventeen years, and yes, that meant seventeen consecutive Christmas parties where she watched him, and encouraged him, to dance with other women. As we continued our training, her dance skill and confidence seemed to grow in equal proportion, and, before long, it was time for her to cross another dance hurdle. Little did I know, she was going to light that hurdle on fire.

I asked her to perform a couple of dance routines at our Studio Showcase, an evening recital that was held twice a year that students of all levels prepared for. This would help solidify her technique and style, but most importantly, it would instill confidence in her to dance in front of an audience. She was initially hesitant, but after we talked it through, she understood and signed up. We chose Frank Sinatra's "I Concentrate on You" for her rumba as a tribute to her husband, who she hoped would get a chance to watch her perform one day. We danced to "Fly Me to the Moon" for her foxtrot. Both dances would prepare her for her night of dancing at her husband's Christmas party.

The next day, she was more jubilant than ever: half walking, half skipping through the doorway and across the dance floor. She was beaming, and it was so gratifying to see how far she'd come. "My husband's coming home!" He would probably be home in a few weeks, she said, but he would try to make it home for her dance performance. At this point, I felt as if I were more nervous than she was. Before long, that would be all but guaranteed.

We rehearsed every day, even on the day of the performance. She was so familiar with the routine that she could hum the song as she danced, and she was even able to show some great style for her dance level. By this point, she wasn't just someone who looked comfortable, she looked confident. She began to dress differently, laugh openly, and on the evening of the event, I'm happy to say that the shy housewife I had first met was nowhere to be found.

As the event began, I scanned the audience for signs of her husband. When it was our turn to perform our foxtrot, we took our places and the signature high-hat of the percussion cued in "Fly Me to the Moon." Shelley was nervous, not unlike any other first-time student. The quiver returned to her smile, but she *was* smiling and dancing like a dream.

When she finished her dance, she took a bow and officially entered a new stage in her confidence. I couldn't have been prouder.

Seating at our Studio Showcases was always limited, so we'd become accustomed to a half dozen or so latecomers accumulating in the doorway to watch our events. Then I noticed someone in our standing room doorway. It was a man, with two large suitcases and a pair of eyeglasses whose reflection that felt like the high beams of a car. So when the orchestration began for "I Concentrate on You," I knew deep down that this was him, her husband. This was the big moment, and this time, it was my smile that was quivering. While Shelley was having the performance moment of her life, I was distracted. Every glance I made toward him, there was no expression on his face. Uh oh. As we neared the end of the routine, I began to wonder, *Is he going to be angry? Will he pull the plug on her dance hobby? Will he take me down with a karate move?* We got through the routine and it was, by my account, a wonderful success. But that feeling had an asterisk, a black-belted, laser-eyed, suitcase-toting asterisk.

The event wrapped up and students were receiving congratulations from their guests. Toward the middle of the dance floor I saw Shelley, her daughter, and her husband. Shelley noticed me and motioned for her husband to come and meet me. He turned, looked at me, and began walking over with the expression of someone entering a business negotiation. "Are you Chris?" he asked before Shelley had a chance to introduce me. My brain's fight-or-flight reflexes had no time to consider an alternate strategy. For a split second, I had this sensation of dread wash over me, that all this work offended him in some way, and that Shelley wouldn't be taking any more dance lessons. Then he reached out his hand; I looked down, returned the gesture, and shook it. He locked eyes with me and said, grinning, "Thank you for making my wife so sexy." I let out a relieved sigh. Then he said, still shaking my hand, "Now I need to sign up for lessons, since she's so much better than me."

It's safe to say that they danced together at the next company Christmas party, and many more after that. I was fortunate enough to watch this one brave move on the part of Shelley become a life-changing moment for her marriage—and for herself. The Backstory you discover is as fulfilling to the professional as it is for the client.

Unfortunately, in the movie that is customer service, there are times when we make our product the star. We turn our customers into flat characters that only seem to move the narrative of our business to the next quarter's returns. The product will eventually be replaced by a newer one and the casting call for more customers will continue.

But what if we changed that approach? If you've learned anything from The Backstory, it's that we must have a relentless curiosity in our customers. By doing so, we turn them into the star of our business narrative. They have depth, they have a story, and let's be honest here, they have a name.

By harnessing the power of The Backstory, you're making your product the supporting character in the narrative of your customer's life.

CHAPTER 3

The Negative

THE NEGATIVE IN ACTION

Think of how many times you've heard a recommendation, seen it coming a mile away, and turned it down. Whether we're buying software or sneakers, we all have a reflexive response to decline an offer. Maybe it's a polite "no thank you" or my personal favorite, "I'd love to, but my wife is the chief financial officer in the family." Many well-intentioned sales presentations have met their demise by these responses, but one pro disarmed me and taught me the power of using a cautionary tale to creative a positive conclusion.

My wife and I were headed to Phoenix for a weekend of dance training with our coaches. We'd gone through the process enough that we had the entire sequence of events down like, well, a dance routine. The first stop was renting a car.

The standard procedure at the car rental counter was to find the cheapest car as quickly as possible and to decline any offers, add-ons, or upgrades. The question, "Do you want to purchase any additional coverage on the vehicle?" would meet a swift demise with our standard "no thanks, it's covered through our credit card" response. That is, until one fateful day.

Behind the counter was a bright-eyed guy in his mid-twenties with his uniform polo shirt tucked in and without a crease in sight. Let's call him James. James greeted us as if he were the owner of the agency, starting with a sincere "Thank you for choosing us!" instead of an empty "How can I help you?" We went through our normal routine: small car, no frills, and as quickly as possible. And then he said something that I'll never forget.

"I'm sure your credit card probably covers you for the insurance, but we recently had a guy pull out into the intersection out front, and he got T-boned by a big truck," he said. Our eyebrows revealed our shock as he continued, "Yeah, I know. Crazy. Anyway, the worst part was that his credit card only covered him for a portion of the damage. He ended up in the hospital and was still on the hook for over twenty thousand." The words "captive audience" and "rental car agent" rarely go together, but James was the exception. "I'd hate for something like that to happen to you guys," he continued, "but if spending a few extra dollars can help you avoid something like that, I'd definitely recommend it." We were sold.

Were we in imminent danger? Probably not. Was James a great customer service representative? You better believe it. We didn't just buy the insurance; we bought his conviction, his interest, and his presentation. I can't say that I've purchased rental car insurance since then, and fortunately we've never had an accident, but I'm sure that James is out there somewhere giving a keynote speech as a champion trainer to future rental car agents.

HOW THE NEGATIVE WORKS

Imagine two roads that your client can take. Your goal is to clearly explain the option you want them to avoid, highlight the option that will work best, and stake your professional reputation on the recommendation.

Clearly Explain the Negative Option

You'd never want someone to catch you choking and say over the loudspeaker, "If any of you are sort of interested in maybe helping out, we are kind of looking for a doctor…." The goal of this skill is to use descriptive words that leave no room for interpretation. Two examples are the phrases "I would hate" and "the last thing I'd want."

Here are some examples:

> I would hate for you to end up with a venue that doesn't accommodate your wedding reception.

> The last thing I'd want is for you to buy the right brand but with the wrong fit.

> I would hate for you to put this off, stress about the deadline, and not enjoy the experience.

> The last thing I'd want is for you to have the right goal but with the wrong strategy.

Highlight the Option That Will Work Best

Giving someone a cautionary tale without an alternative plan is about as pleasant as your personal trainer explaining that you're overweight but then refusing to let you exercise. A problem needs a solution like a carb-loving author needs a workout program. So, let's take a look at some ways to transition from the cautionary path to the better option. As you practice this skill, think of these transitional phrases as the shift from one path to the other.

Here's What I'm Thinking

The last thing I'd want is for you to meet the right guy but during the wrong dance, so here's what I'm thinking: let's focus on some of the new dances in your next few lessons.

The last thing I'd want is for you to buy the right brand but with the wrong fit, so here's what I'm thinking: let's take five minutes to get you sized correctly and then you can shop without worrying.

Here's What We're Going to Do

I'd hate for you to come all this way only to be stuck waiting for your hotel room, so here's what we're going to do: let's check in your bags, and I'd like to give you this voucher for one of our world-famous cocktails on the house.

The last thing I'd want is for a scheduling issue to stand in the way of a great experience, so here's what we're going to do: I'm going to move mountains to make sure you get something as close as possible to your preferred time.

Notice the trend? The clear problem (I would hate…), connected by a transition (here's what…), followed by a beneficial solution (I'm going to move mountains) completes your customer service cautionary tale, also known as The Negative.

Requirements for The Negative

Being negative doesn't take much work. Just watch any reality show and see how long it lasts before someone is complaining. Presenting The Negative in a customer service environment will take some effort, but it will create results even a reality television star could appreciate.

1. Empathy for Your Client: Is your client on a service trajectory that won't deliver a desirable result? Imagining the end result, the pain they may experience, the inconvenience of a poor choice, or the frustration that combusts when good intentions combine with a bad strategy are available to you if you're willing to look through the eyes of your customer. If it were you as the consumer, what would you hope a great service professional would say?

2. The First Right of Refusal: Silence might be golden in a movie theater, but it is also agreement in any conversational framework. If a woman asks her husband, "Do I look fat in this dress?" that silence might also be deadly. If you are silent, sitting and watching as your product is reduced to diminishing levels of enjoyment to your client, you become part of the problem. To deliver The Negative, it is imperative that you give your client the first right of refusal. Meaning: lay out your presentation, present the options, and let them make an informed decision. Even if they decline, at the very least, you can establish your position as a professional looking out for their best interests.

3. Firm Belief in Your Product: In the fantasy world of comic books and movies, some superpowers are used for evil instead of good. The Negative is no different. A poor customer service representative could use this same framework to encourage a client to leave a company, reveal a lack of belief in their product, and look for a better deal elsewhere. To use The Negative correctly, a service professional needs to have an unwavering belief in their product. After all, this conversation is a detour from the norm, a

challenge to the status quo, and the customer service equivalent to swimming upstream.

Tips for Finding the Negative

Congratulations! You are now an official customer service detective, undeterred by the challenge, finding a story in the faintest of clues. Every crime against service is a classroom. The following is a true story for you to investigate, in which a great customer service opportunity met an untimely end. Using what you know about The Negative, where would you insert an alternate route to recalibrate the customer toward a better result?

THE HOUSE KILLER

"Wait, what?" was my first response when I got the news. The president of our company had invited me and some friends to golf with him at his home course in Florida. I was thrilled at the opportunity to rub elbows with the head honcho; it felt like I was going to be living out that scene from *Big* where Tom Hanks' character ends up making some suggestions to a guy that turns out to be the owner of the company. They hit it off, and then they play chopsticks together on a huge floor piano to affirm their bond. This would be the golf version of that. The only problem? I am a horrible golfer.

While there are plenty of people in the world that probably share that same sentiment, let me give you some insight. My friends (and they certainly earned that title if they chose to golf with me) referred to a certain club in my bag as "the House Killer." Why, you ask? Because any time I used that club, my ball would find its way to the side of a home. Of somebody who probably paid an extra half-million just to have the House Killer ruin their day and insurance premiums.

So I did what any self-respecting bad golfer would do if they had a house killer in their bag and a big golf date on the schedule: I signed up for lessons. I didn't want to take any chances and have my house killer club show up unannounced on my big golfing day. So, I sought out the very best teacher I could find. After a search of "top golf teachers in the Bay Area," I found the teacher for me. He was the highest-rated professional in my area, and even with an hour commute to see him before work, I knew it would be worth the extra effort. Golf chopsticks was in my sights and this teacher would calibrate my aim.

But all of that would change the moment I arrived at the facility that foggy morning. I got cold feet and started convincing myself that golf wasn't something I really needed in my life (if you read the preface already, it was a lot like that). But this time, I called my wife in a desperate attempt to validate my retreat: "Hey babe, do you think it's a good idea for me to drive all the way out here for golf lessons if there's other work I could be doing?"

But she saw right through my flimsy attempt: "Listen to yourself. You *need* golf lessons." She emphasized need like she was recommending clothes to a nude toddler on their way to greet the neighbors. "Besides," she continued, "where do you work?"

"Arthur Murray Dance Studios," I mumbled.

"That's right. You help people do this with their dancing all the time. So, what are you worried about?" Her approach was the motivational equivalent of a heat-seeking missile, and she had me in the crosshairs.

My response back was also an admission of guilt: "I just feel like I'm going to be the worst person there."

Then she said exactly what I needed to hear but hoped she would avoid: "That's why you take lessons. You don't start them after you're good." My inner narrator added, *You start them when you suck, just like you*, but she interrupted him by reminding me to call her when it was done and telling me she was proud of me for going for it.

I unloaded my clubs, eyeing my House Killer as I lugged them all to the front desk of the golf training center. The interior wasn't lavish. There were posted rates up above the desk like a coffee shop menu and different golf characters milling around. No obvious beacons of reassurance for my poor golf skills. Maybe it was my nerves muting my senses, but it may as well have been a coffee shop with one employee behind the counter.

Eventually, my golf teacher was introduced to me. Let's call him George. "So how would you rate your golf game?" he asked. I shared with him a detailed account of my poor play, the entire history of the House Killer, and the opportunity to play with the president. He had, I explained to him, "five months to turn me into a great golfer."

He didn't seem fazed by my story in the slightest. In fact, he got right down to business and explained the next step in our introductory lesson: "I'm going to record your swing and then we're going to look at it side by side with a PGA pro." If you've ever hated listening to the sound of your own voice, there is a level of torture far worse, and that's watching a video of yourself swinging a golf club in a side-by-side comparison with a professional. But, as I kept telling myself, it was all for the greater good.

I try to use humor whenever I can to lighten the mood. If I'm out of my normal element, it's my go-to to create a connection with those around me. So, once we finished our video exam torture session, I asked George, "Okay, doctor...is there any hope for me?" He gave me a polite smile you might use when someone gives you unsolicited advice, then led me up some stairs to the second level of a very busy driving range. It was a cold, weekday mid-morning and, just to complete my nightmare scenario, it was the most happening spot in town. Ping! Golf balls were rocketing away from golfers much more equipped than I was, but I still had hope. My teacher was my saving grace, or so I hoped.

We stopped at our reserved stall and I set my clubs down. As I looked at the House Killer, I attempted to connect with George again: "Okay, so should we start with the House Killer? You're the expert, of course, but that would be great."

He gave a half version of his earlier smile and responded, "Let's start with your six-iron." He pulled out a bucket of balls, gave me some light instruction, and then asked me to hit all the balls in the basket. In my attempt to be a model student, I dutifully followed each tip he had given me. For every five to seven bad swings I had, there was at least one halfway decent one. But there were exactly zero responses from my expert teacher. In my mind's eye, he was examining my movements, studying my form, looking for areas of improvement and establishing a strategy to make me the golfer of my dreams. As I was loading up the final ball in the basket, I turned back to him to get a status report.

The only analysis taking place was him scrolling through his BlackBerry. "Okay, so what's next?" I asked. He handed me another bucket of balls and had me repeat the exercise. Each hack of my six-iron seemed to push me further away from my goal. The lesson was like a reality show bad date that was doomed from the start. But my desire to become a better golfer seemed to withstand every disinterested moment with George.

This came to its zenith when we returned to the front desk. I understood the procedure and wanted to make it as seamless as possible. I was there on a trial lesson, and this was the moment when George would recommend the best strategy for me to continue taking lessons, and then I'd buy some. But he didn't recommend anything. He just stood there, like a trick or treater that wouldn't leave the porch after getting a handful of candy. In a desperate move, I broke the ice: "So I guess I need to get one of these packages of lessons, right?"

He shrugged, "Yeah, if you want to." I felt like I was being dumped.

I gestured to the top package, just to show him my commitment: "What about that ten-package?"

His response was yet another diminishing return on my effort to take lessons: "If that's what you want to do."

I'd love to tell you that he snapped out of it, slapped his hand on the desk, leaned in close and told me exactly how I would get to a point where my golf game wasn't the butt of the joke with my friends. That he spoke from the heart, laid out a plan, regardless of the cost, because he believed in the value of the investment. But it should come as no surprise that he didn't do any of this. I'd also love to tell you that I didn't sign up for the most expensive package just to teach the guy a lesson, but I can't.

I showed up for one more lesson, then no more. George was the same, my golf game was the same, and the round of golf with the president never materialized.

Analysis

So, how did you do? If you had been in George's shoes, knowing what you know now, what would you have said to help create a positive solution? As counterintuitive as it may sound, The Negative is an incredible tool for creating positive solutions. Going with the flow, as with our friend George, has just the opposite result.

CHAPTER 4

Muscle Memory

Rethink the phrase "proof of progress" and call it what it really is: "proof of value." Without progress, there is no value. Whether it's a new home being constructed or a new golf swing, it would be harder to justify the investment if progress can't be measured. That's where Muscle Memory comes in, our fourth basic component of the Customer Service Choreography.

In dancing, that measurable proof of progress comes in the form of Muscle Memory. It's our mile marker, like the first inches lost in a fitness program or the first dividends on an investment. Without it, our product can be nothing more than a speculative idea, like an impulse purchase. Until Muscle Memory is communicated and created, the idea will continue to have diminishing value; however, when Muscle Memory is accounted for, it can accelerate the activity into an investment with an exponential return.

Muscle Memory allows a new dancer to maneuver like a seasoned driver would on the open road. Without the burden of nerves, overthinking, or frustration, it creates the closest thing to "dancing autopilot."

The payoff is a surge in enthusiasm, momentum in the learning process, and trust in our curriculum. Whether it's called a breakthrough, a lightbulb moment, or the day the cherubs of learning rejoice and blow their trumpets, these are all just connotations for what's really at work: Muscle Memory.

Muscle Memory, as the term might imply, isn't just something we talk about. It must be constructed with a series of methods and pressure tested to ensure it holds. The best part? This works in other industries, even if your product isn't super sweet dance moves.

SO HOW CAN MUSCLE MEMORY HELP CREATE BETTER CUSTOMER SERVICE?

Muscle Memory as Checkpoints in the Buyer's Journey

Imagine this scene as if it were in the bordered panels of a comic book: A salesclerk holds up a pair of sneakers; the tilt of his head and shrug of his shoulders say, "How about these?" In the next panel, a young customer's eyes widen: "These are the ones I've been looking for," they say. The clerk hands the young shopper the selection. It looks like the sneaker equivalent of a tea ceremony. They smile through the exchange, and both look pleased with the outcome. In the final panel, the clerk proudly watches on as his young shopper exits the store, with the "squeak-squeak" sound emanating from the soles of his new purchase.

If customer service is made up of peaks and valleys, that scene would definitely be the peak. Whether you sell sneakers or stock options, it feels great to have your clients find what they are looking for, listen to your recommendation, and leave your place of business better than when they first arrived. Unfortunately, that isn't always the case. So, let's talk about valleys.

If a peak is a satisfied customer, a valley is buyer's remorse. In our sneaker comic story, this would play out with our young sneaker shopper returning to the store, avoiding eye contact with the salesclerk, holding his receipt in one hand and his boxed shoes in the other, and asking for his money back. The clerk might even show a subtle tinge of betrayal watching this—a heavy sigh, a tightening of the lips, or an eye roll as he heads back to the stockroom. Over time, if this scene was repeated with different customers, you might expect our salesclerk's enthusiasm to wane. Not all at once, of course, but an imperceptible descent, reducing one degree at a time from committing himself to great service. If a sale is a type of relationship between the customer and the associate, then it would be natural for the clerk to feel a little guarded if he had been dumped a few times. But let's examine this closer and see how Muscle Memory can help.

GUIDING THE JOURNEY

Think of Muscle Memory as the milestones on a customer's journey. Whether that's a journey with a product you send your client off with or a continued experience with you along the way, this skill isn't just touting the benefits of a product to achieve a transaction. It's about how the product should be used to achieve the best possible results. The choreography of Muscle Memory should:

1. Share the benchmarks of achievement you want your client to reach.
2. Build evidence for measurable proof of progress.
3. Insulate your customer from buyer's remorse.
4. Ensure that your product has lasting value and is not just a quick sale.

Our shoe salesman might have said, "These sneakers run a little tight but will stretch to your size and fit like a glove if you're okay with them feeling snug for the first couple of days." This way, our young shopper wouldn't have been surprised by the fit of his shoes, regretted the purchase, and returned them. Our salesperson wouldn't have seethed under his breath or let this interaction erode the joy in his work. Muscle Memory doesn't bask in the glow of the transaction; it guides the client past the purchase, helps pinpoint obstacles, and directs the experience toward the intended results.

If you worked at a driving school, Muscle Memory would be the moment your pupil could drive and talk simultaneously. You'd emphasize the goal, describe the practical benefits once it is achieved, and this would, in turn, validate the process you'd go through to achieve it. For example, you might say something like, "A driver isn't just someone who knows the mechanics of how to drive. It's someone that can drive with friends in the car, with the music on, not worrying about where their hands go. To do that, we're going to develop your muscle memory."

A great massage therapist will remind you to drink plenty of cucumber-infused water after a treatment; a realtor will remind you that your new house might not feel like a home until you've thrown your first dinner party; and your doctor will, undoubtedly, prescribe plenty of milestones for you to maintain your health.

Out of all of our core Customer Service Choreography components so far—The Secret Mission, The Negative, The Backstory—Muscle Memory can easily come across as the most "dancey" of the bunch. To help add clarity to any type of industry—and because, as mentioned earlier, Muscle Memory is a process—we are going to cover four ways to implement Muscle Memory.

1. The Blueprint of Muscle Memory: How to project and communicate the milestones for your customer's journey
2. The Challenge of Muscle Memory: How challenges can establish value in your product and professional credibility

3. The Evidence of Muscle Memory: How to use progress to build belief, and a better compliment
4. The Implementation Muscle Memory: How to talk about Muscle Memory with your clients

1. The Blueprint of Muscle Memory

If the customer journey was a long, dark road, then this section is about turning on the thoughtfully placed streetlights. The Blueprint of Muscle Memory gives the beginning of a new product journey a target that is measured, clearly explained, and within reach. Here's an example:

With my pen, I circled the very last square on the page. There were twelve total, but the last one, number twelve, got the circle. Each of the squares was a small area for notes for each private dance lesson. Considering my students, I knew that by number twelve, things would be a whole lot different. "This is the point," I motioned to the circle, "where we will have our first big breakthrough." My students, Karl and Stephanie, had tried dance lessons once before but had run into some difficulty. They began with group classes at the local rec center to no avail. To them, dancing was a romantic excursion and a chance to connect on a deeper level. Instead, they were drifting in a sea of people, lost without any personalized instruction, and their great date night idea was sunk. That is, until they drove by Arthur Murray.

This new dance program, the one with the now-circled twelfth square, was their first time taking private lessons. The individual instruction changed everything for them. "That's usually the point where muscle memory starts kicking in," I said, "and stuff like talking and dancing is less of a challenge." They brightened. Then I added, "Smiling and breathing are just a bonus." Karl and Stephanie began this program with the normal struggles that come with new dance couples. If you think about it, dancing with a partner is learning a new, non-verbal language. As with any form of communication, there can be misunderstandings. On the dance floor, those come in the form of a few toes getting stepped on from time to time. But, eventually, we reached that first milestone. On that fateful day, where the cherubs of progress seemed to sing out from the acoustic ceiling panels, Karl and Stephanie danced an entire lap of foxtrot around the dance floor.

Karl's look could best be described as a combination of exhilaration and disbelief, like he had just skydived for the first time. Stephanie's response was a gradual crescendo. From halfway through the lap, her faced revealed a sense of wide-eyed recognition that Karl was, in fact, totally in control. As a confident woman, not shy at all about offering feedback in earlier lessons, she stayed quiet and seemed to beam brighter the further they went around the floor. By the end, she burst out, "Honey, you did it!" I watched as she looked at her husband, as if seeing him with some renewed perspective. The best part? This all happened by lesson number ten.

That simple circle, combined with that circle around the dance floor, was my first Muscle Memory blueprint, and it wouldn't be my last. That moment changed the way I taught my students forever. Sure, the circle might be on a different number, there might have been a few times where I used a highlighter or colored pencil, but the message was the same: This is my estimate for our first breakthrough. This is where your dancing will start to feel comfortable. This was the Blueprint of Muscle Memory.

The old adage is to under-promise and over-deliver. Unfortunately, since this adage is well known to most people—especially when it comes to projections and timelines for a process—many professionals opt to not promise a thing. This way, on paper, no one is disappointed, but nothing could be further from the truth. With Karl and Stephanie, the promise is what gave our time its purpose. It laid the blueprint so they understood that there was, in fact, a process. When your client understands the process, then they can celebrate the achievement.

The Blueprint:
Promise + Purpose + Process = Achievement

Marathon Training

One of our students, Tim, shared a story with me about a group he was training with to run a marathon: 26.2 miles, to be exact. "We found a long stretch of road and we'd drive up and leave water bottles every three miles," he said. "Then we'd run to each water bottle, take a break, and run to the next. Eventually, we started skipping the breaks and setting the water out farther and farther." I was consumed by the training elements of this story. The water bottles were the milestones, a clear way to gauge progress, and psychologically, a shorter goal to run for than the entire 26.2 miles. I was captivated by this brilliant approach. This was the Blueprint of Muscle Memory in action. I have yet to run a marathon myself, but you can bet I'll try this water bottle training to prepare.

I firmly believe that the best breakthroughs are the ones that drive you crazy for not learning them sooner. Upon reflection, prior to Karl and Stephanie's breakthrough, I never had that kind of Blueprint strategy. I never made any promises, and I never clarified the milestones. My strategy could best be described as hoping for the best and holding my breath. I was operating on a limited lesson-to-lesson window. My dance programs were like marathons but without any intermediate goals or expectations communicated; there were no water bottles at predefined checkmarks. As a result, the path to their improvement would become compromised. This came in the form of canceled appointments or discontinued dance programs. The breath-holding, scared-new-teacher version of me couldn't pinpoint the root cause, and I lost some great students because of it. I was asking them to run a marathon to train for a marathon instead of breaking that up into smaller increments that would reveal their progress. Karl and Stephanie may have had a dance breakthrough but, on the same day, I celebrated an important teaching breakthrough.

My mission after that was to repeat the process with everyone. I decided to make the Blueprint a regular part of my student interactions. I was determined to take the feelings of forehead-slapping regret and transform it into my fuel for any students I had going forward.

If I hadn't, then Sarah's story would have slipped right past me.

A Muscle Memory Success Story

When Sarah first came in, I never would have guessed that she was out of place. She was enthusiastic, outgoing, and loud, but what can you expect from a tenth grader? Sarah's parents wanted her to have a hobby that would have some long-term social benefits. Like many high schoolers, she needed some help in the posture department. As her teacher, I asked her questions to get to know what she wanted to achieve outside of just the dance moves. "I just want to fit in," she said, "I don't really have a crowd." Here was a bubbly and engaging high schooler without a tribe to share those traits with. She had a wide, dynamic range of confidence; she was great with people she knew but shrunk away from people she didn't.

We worked on all the fun dances that seemed to be tailor-made for her personality: the swing, the cha-cha, and the salsa. Each of these dances had fun music, a fast pace, and Sarah poured herself into each one like a voracious reader with one tattered book to their name that steps into a library for the first time. I'd taught people before who came in as a gift from someone else. It was usually the dance lesson equivalent of wearing that scratchy sweater grandma knitted for you at least once, while she was visiting, before it was put into permanent storage.

But Sarah was much different. From my vantage point, Sarah had either been so vocal about her goal to become a ballroom dancer or her parents happened to hit the jackpot grand prize of gift-giving.

Rather than continue with the dances she was so drawn toward, I opted to expand her repertoire with dances that would improve her poise, balance, and posture. This began with the foxtrot, then the tango, and finally, the waltz. These more classic dances can, in some cases, be the equivalent of suggesting a nice multivitamin as an alternative to dessert, but I believed in her benefits and decided to share the idea with her.

"You probably won't use the waltz and tango at a school dance because that's not what they are designed for," I said. "Really, they are there to give you the look of a dancer, even when you aren't dancing." She seemed to consider it silently, then I added, "Not to mention, your parents will be happy you're learning some of the elegant stuff." So she agreed, and we set her dance plans in motion. On her next lesson, just as I'd done with Karl and Stephanie, we started the with a clear Blueprint for her Muscle Memory.

"Sarah, our plan is to attack your fun dances and posture dances equally. At some point, if someone outside the studio notices that you're standing taller, tell me, because that's how we'll know it's working." I circled a few lesson checkpoints for some of our goals: "By this point, we will have all of the dances introduced" and "by this point, we will start talking about doing a performance." But the big one was posture; it was the one, critical bit of physical proof of progress that she carried with her in everyday life.

Sarah danced through the summer that year. She made progress in leaps and bounds, not just because of her physical ability but because of her outlook. She was such a grateful learner. The ballroom dances, with heavy emphasis on posture, were definitely showing up in her balance and how she carried herself. It was as if her neck got longer, in a good way, or she was going through a growth spurt. Developing this into the physical form of Muscle Memory required a lot of repetition. Fortunately, the variety of dances allowed the posture improvement to be spread over a variety of inputs—like switching from the waltz to the swing. Eventually, every dance became a posture dance.

When the new school year rolled around, she shared that she was thinking of auditioning for a role in a school theater production. I was thrilled to hear it. It had been a secret goal of hers, but she had never had the confidence to pursue it. The moment she shared it, I felt like her talent agent and older brother combined into one. "You have to do it," I said, "you'll be perfect for that!" Theater. It was perfect. It was like a puzzle piece you couldn't quite fit until you examined it from the other side of the table. I could see her fitting in perfectly with the theater kids. So we incorporated that into our conversations on our lessons. I wanted to know as much about that as possible so I could coach her and lend a motivational word if necessary. Despite her bigger academic load—junior year can be tricky—Sarah kept up with her dancing, stayed on top of each milestone we set out, and she was a regular, more confident part of our dance studio community.

A couple weeks later, she rushed into her lesson smiling, but fighting back tears. "It happened!" she said, the words bursting out with a half laugh, half sob. "Just like you said!"

My eyes widened. "What happened?" I asked, worried that something awful had happened. But aside from the tears in her eyes, she looked positive and animated.

"It was incredible," she said, lifting the weight of worry I was carrying, "I don't know if I got it yet, but listen to this," she pushed the sob in her voice down to articulate. "They asked me how long I had been a dancer." She shared it with the excitement of a parent telling their kids they are going on a surprise trip to Disneyland. She continued, "I walked out on stage, and before I said anything, the director asked me how long I'd been a dancer," she continued. "They said they could see it from a mile away."

Sarah got the role. She also had no problem in the confidence department when she danced at our local dance events—thanks, Muscle Memory—and I continued to teach her until she finished high school. Part of me still feels a little like that older brother and talent agent. Sure, she was an absolute delight to teach, but witnessing her benefits materialize into a life-changing reality is the reason I smile any time I think of her story.

Takeaway: Visual Evidence is vital to building Muscle Memory and successful Blueprints. In your industry, what are the key visual clues that would be easy to spot that could serve as evidence? Lock in and communicate them, and your customer's belief in you will grow (along with the lifespan of their time with your product).

2. The Challenge of Muscle Memory

Earlier in the chapter, our shoe salesman story highlighted the need for mapping out the customer journey and that Muscle Memory is about both the peaks and the valleys. This section is about the valleys, or challenges, that the customer will face. The best customer service professionals know that the sooner you can communicate them, the sooner you can reduce their negative impact. Leaving those challenges to chance is a recipe for buyer's remorse, and it's the sign of a customer service representative that hasn't reached their full potential. A professional isn't threatened by inherent challenges in the buyer's journey. Each challenge presents an opportunity to showcase how the product and the professional can help the customer overcome the obstacles that will occur. In doing so, customer can feel success, the professional can be the guide, and the product can become the hero. While this may all sound like some strange customer service version of an adventure movie, you can find examples of this hidden in everyday life. For example:

You're flying home from a business trip. It's early enough that you're savoring your watered-down cup of airline coffee, hoping beyond hope that it can give you the jolt that you need to feel functional. What you could really use is a little blood circulation, so you set your coffee in the small divot in your seat-back tray and "excuse me" your way past your fellow passenger, better known as the gatekeeper in the aisle seat. Your body groans and pops like an old engine starting up and, just as you're stepping toward the bathroom, there's an announcement over the cabin loudspeaker: "Ladies and gentlemen, this is your captain speaking. We are coming toward a little turbulence. If you could please return to your seats, the Fasten Seatbelt sign is now illuminated."

The signs above everyone's seat light up; the ding of the prompt is mixed with the metal-on-metal sounds of the lap seatbelts. Whether it's the interrupted stretch break or the fact that the flight feels completely calm, you are a little irritated as you make your way back to your window seat. Just as you're preparing a jeering remark about the captain to your aisle-mate, it happens: turbulence. And not just a mild case—the kind of turbulence that would have splashed that watered-down coffee all over your business suit. But you got the warning: You're wearing your seatbelt, and what's left of your coffee is sloshing inside the Styrofoam cup with the airplane embossed on its side. Even better, you're wide awake now.

A great pilot will inform the passengers and make adjustments before turbulence arrives. Even if it's frustrating or inconvenient to you as a passenger, the pilot is still obligated to share the information with you as the professional. It's part and parcel with their training, entrenched in their professional identity, they will do whatever it takes to help you arrive safely at your destination (even if that's inconvenient for you at times).

Interestingly enough, when the turbulence does hit, it's hard not to reserve a small mental tip of the cap in recognition of the pilot's expertise. Conversely, imagine a flight where the pilot doesn't provide those updates. Imagine the backlash of passengers experiencing turbulence, with the pilot adding insult to injury with a delayed announcement: "It looks like we are experiencing turbulence." That pilot would sound like a buffoon. The moral of the story is simple: Any amateur can find problems as they are happening. Average professionals will let their personal feelings stop them from performing the job their customers expect, but a great professional informs their customers before there's a problem.

This isn't to suggest that you share problems with your customers without a solution. The pilot didn't announce, "Hey, there's going to be turbulence and I have no idea what to do. Can someone help?" Being clear about the adversity is one thing, but being capable of resolving the issue is another. So let's see where we're at here. The pilot makes the announcement of a potential problem (turbulence) and it's typically met with casual belief, if you will. From there, when the turbulence does happen, it confirms the announcement, eliminates any disbelief, and could, quite easily, cause some anxiety. Finally, when the pilot guides the passengers past the issue, your appreciation for their skill is greater; they led you, and your fellow passengers, past the problem.

So where are the expected bumps in the journey with your product? Can you pinpoint them? Better yet, do you have a solution to limit the bumps? We've all heard the time-honored classic sales quote of, "the sale begins when the buyer says no." It is the mantra for sales-oriented professionals. The idea is to use persistence to wear down resistance, to pull out all the stops in a negotiation, and to reframe a negative response into the beginning, not the end. So why don't we create something similar for customer service? If "the sale begins when the buyer says no," then "the service begins when the buyer says yes."

This means that even if the sale has been made, we aren't finished. We will use our persistence to wear down the resistance they may be facing, we will pull out all the stops when delivering our service, and we won't see a negative response as an ending—just the beginning of a new layer of our expertise.

Even, and especially, if that includes some challenges along the way.

3. The Evidence of Muscle Memory

We live in a world where people can treat positive feedback and negative comments with equal amounts of skepticism. A great customer service professional understands that a compliment without evidence is like a sports car without wheels; it may look nice, but it won't go anywhere.

In this area of our Muscle Memory training, let's look at the challenges of delivering great feedback and the tools for providing enough evidence for a compliment to make a lasting impression.

Imagine a road trip to a popular theme park with your family. After hours of kids' music, emergency bathroom breaks, and over one hundred "are we there yet?" questions, you arrive. You exhale a weary sigh, imagine a cocktail and a shower in your future, and announce, "We're here!" And that's when three words jab you like a stray Lego into your bare feet.

"No, we're not," the critic in the booster seat (better known as your four-year-old) says. As if nullifying the bleary-eyed miles you gutted out on behalf of your family vacation, you dismiss it as a joke. "No, look, honey, it's just dark. This is the hotel," you say. "No, this isn't the park," she counters. So, like any tired, but rational, adult, you blurt out a quick laugh (the preamble to a loss of sanity), douse the flames of fury with a cleansing breath, and unpack your family from the vehicle.

This isn't an argument you need to win. For now, you've stated your case, you agree to disagree with the four-year-old, and you have faith that the entrance to the theme park will wash away any evidence of disbelief from your skeptical passenger.

If progress were a real place, there would be plenty of visitors who would claim it wasn't. While this place called progress should be an awakening, a full-circle moment filled with appreciation of a well-earned result, skepticism can unfortunately have far-reaching effects. Even with sincere praise from the most well-intentioned professionals, skepticism can diminish the validity of compliments faster than you can say "imposter syndrome." Whether it's your mom telling you you're gorgeous or your dance teacher sharing how much you've improved in your salsa, a "you're just telling me that because you're supposed to" can feel like the service equivalent of landing on the "go directly to jail" square in Monopoly.

It doesn't matter what the industry is; there will always be a client that is hard to compliment, not because of their deservedness but because of their skepticism. As the professional, you have a vested interest in helping the customer achieve a great result, but even if you are honest and sincere about it, you may not know the entire Backstory. There may have been a poor customer service moment in their past that you'll need to rise beyond. If you think about it, you've been that customer before, haven't you?

Maybe you tried on a new shirt and had to fight off a big eye roll when the clerk said, "Oh, that looks so great on you." Or you cringed, put your head down, and speed walked through the mall, past all the kiosks of sales reps telling you how beautiful you are and how their product can enhance it. Unearned praise feels like a tactic, like something that person would never say to you outside of that setting. As consumers we come away wondering more about what they have to gain in terms of commission than what we had to gain by purchasing the product. So, how can customer service professionals get past this?

With irrefutable evidence.

Time + Distance

Subjective evidence ("You look so great in that") is all opinion-based. It's easy to discard. Think of the last time you heard a parent or grandparent tell you how handsome or beautiful you are. Sure, it feels nice, but it can also leave you muttering under your breath, "You're supposed to say that!" On the other hand, objective evidence is rooted in facts, things that you can measure, changes that you can see, hold, and compare. If your mother said, "You've grown so much this year," it would be hard to shrug that off, especially if you can see the wall in your house with lines, dates, and notches displaying your proof of progress.

With dancing, we love to use time and distance challenges to demonstrate the evidence of Muscle Memory. In this case, a student, let's call him Mr. Jones, is new to dancing. We are expecting him to be skeptical of any praise. Any attempt to verbally convince him of his ability only stacks more weight on the scales of skepticism, rationalized by pointing out the compliment as self-serving for the teacher and not deserving of the student: "You just say that because you're supposed to."

Instead of campaigning for the validity of any praise, we'll take an evidence-building approach to allow Mr. Jones to draw his own conclusions.

"Mr. Jones, on today's lesson, muscle memory is the name of the game. Our first mission, should you choose to accept it, is to dance the tango for one minute, without stopping, while carrying on a conversation." Sixty seconds may not seem like much, but talking while dancing can feel like carrying a conversation while parallel parking; it takes some brain processing power.

Just to make it extra real, let's say that Mr. Jones has had some bad customer service interactions in the past. He's far outside the confines of his comfort zone, and that causes him to keep his guard up. With students like Mr. Jones, and many others like him, this Time + Distance challenge works like a charm, but with one added formula: evidence before compliments.

"Mr. Jones, you just finished dancing over a minute, keeping a conversation, and dancing your tango the entire time. What this tells me is that we've just had our first breakthrough with muscle memory. Great job, how did that feel to you?"

If this had been inverted, with the compliment come before the evidence ("Mr. Jones, I think you're a wonderful dancer"), do you think he would have accepted that as sincere praise? Most likely not. It would sound like something a well-intentioned, but self-serving, professional should say because it's their job. But with some concrete proof serving as evidence, an assessment of how the Muscle Memory ties in, and then a dollop of praise, it would be hard for Mr. Jones, or your toughest client, to refute it.

4. The Implementation of Muscle Memory

Now that we understand the fundamentals of Muscle Memory as a part of our customer service choreography, let's put it into action. In this final section, we will zoom in and look at some practical examples of how this can be implemented in a variety of service environments.

1. The Blueprint of Muscle Memory

If your product's total value is at the top of a staircase, then what is the first step to getting there? That's the blueprint.

> Promise: Give your customer your projection for when they can reach a particular stage in the journey.

> Purpose: Remind them of how these steps correspond to their bigger goal.

Process: Explain your process and any steps they can take toward improving upon it.

Here's an example:

Shawn has just purchased a premium software package for his small business, and it includes a dedicated onboarding representative. Stacy is her company's rockstar when it comes to onboarding, not just because she keeps things fun but because she lays out the strategy so well.

Stacy: "Okay, Shawn, I'm so glad you went with our product. Now let's talk strategy, sound good?"

Shawn: "Definitely. I'm all ears."

Stacy: "It can take up to six weeks to get through this onboarding process but, if you're up for it, I think we can do it in half the time. This way, you can have this software in your muscle memory and integrated with your workflow. What do you say?"

Shawn: "Wow, I'd love that."

Stacy: "Great. We'll arrange ninety-minute appointments instead of the standard forty-five, and I'm confident that you'll appreciate taking this approach. Not to mention, we can expect a huge breakthrough within three weeks' time. Let's check out the schedule."

Did you catch her Blueprint?

The Promise: "I think we can do it in half the time."

The Purpose: "We'll have this software in your muscle memory and integrated with your workflow."

The Process: "We'll arrange ninety-minute appointments instead of the standard forty-five."

The purchase of the software may have ended the cycle for the sales department, but it activated Stacy's role in the service of onboarding the client. She laid out the timeframe, pinpointed a feeling, and suggested a strategy to accelerate it. If you were Stacy's client, how would you feel about this suggestion?

Promise + Purpose + Process = Achievement

2. The Challenge of Muscle Memory

When a client is on the service side of their journey, there will be challenges, but your ability to articulate them shouldn't be one of them. While you can't eliminate all the obstacles in their path, your role is to reduce the number of momentum-sapping surprises and utilize the threats as opportunities to add value to their decision to buy your product. Here's an example:

Charlie is a guitar teacher. What started as a passion for transferring his love for the guitar has begun to fade. Lately, any time a music competition show is in season, he sees a seasonal interest in the six-stringed instrument he's so passionate about. So, over time, Charlie's light as a motivator began to dim. He started treating his students with the same expectation; that they'd quit like all the others. When they did, it just validated his opinion. But all of that changed when he met his new student, Lucy.

Lucy's mom shared that her eleven-year-old was a former violin student that preferred her dad's classic rock collection over dolls, makeup, or pop music. This hit Charlie like a Led Zeppelin guitar solo. "This one is different," thought Charlie. "I'm going to help her become great at this."

By the end of the lesson, Charlie decided he did not want Lucy to be anything less than his protégé, even if that meant changing his normal approach.

> Charlie: "Lucy, I want you to know that your goal of becoming a great guitar soloist is my goal too. I want to set up a plan to help get you there so everyone can see what you're capable of and you can see it too. Does that sound good?"

> Lucy: "Yeah, okay."

> Charlie: "Here's the thing; your fingers have to hurt a little bit before you can start shredding those chords we worked on, [to Lucy's mom] but if we can get together a few more times this week, [to both of them] I am confident we can get that into your muscle memory. Are you up for the challenge?"

> Lucy: "Okay. I mean, Mom, is that okay?"

> Lucy's mom: "Of course, sweetie. Charlie, what did you have in mind?"

In the world of Customer Service, there are plenty of Charlies out there. Professionals who have encountered some rejection and let their original passion grow dim in the process. But all it takes is one client to change that. In The Challenge of Muscle Memory, our goal is to repurpose the obstacles and present them as opportunities, not threats. Learning the guitar requires a little discomfort in the beginning, but a professional with commitment can carve, or shred, through that when they communicate the vision.

Thinking of our turbulence story, it would be awful if a pilot withheld the instructions to sit down and fasten seatbelts for fear of being an inconvenience to the audience. The same can be said for any professional where health or safety is on the line. There will be times when you have to share bad news, inconvenient details, or communicate some hard work ahead. But your goal as a customer service professional is to err on the side of invitation

Charlie could have continued with his dim outlook and muted enthusiasm for his students, but he took the bold choice of inviting Lucy to be great, regardless of the challenges.

No one is ever offended by an invitation to improve, even if they can't accept it, but everyone will judge a professional that withholds that opportunity poorly.

Here are the steps to remember:

1. Common Vision: Charlie emphasized the vision Lucy had for herself and validated it.
2. Communicate the Challenge: Charlie was open about the obstacles but with an optimistic outlook.
3. Plan and Invitation: Lucy was invited to take part in Charlie's plan for her.
4. The Challenge of Muscle Memory must account for both the peaks and the valleys in the customer's, and sometimes the professional's, journey.

3. The Evidence of Muscle Memory

Finally, let's examine another application of The Evidence of Muscle Memory. Our goal, if you remember, is to understand that compliments without evidence will rarely stick. As professionals, we should operate under the basic assumption that praise can, and will, come across as self-serving if it isn't communicated correctly, which can disrupt the positive momentum of the connection you are creating. To do this, we can find areas of measurement, like time and distance, that create objective evidence and undeniable proof. Here's an example:

James is a personal trainer and has a soft spot for people struggling with body image. He, himself, lost over one hundred pounds with the help of a new diet and a great trainer who pushed him both physically and mentally. His client, Brandon, exhibited all the telltale signs reminiscent of where James was not too long ago; he wore his clothes extra baggy, had a defeated tone in his voice, and couldn't seem to articulate a vision for his fitness goals beyond just "losing weight."

It's been three weeks since Brandon's first visit, which began as a series of exercises that seemed to have the same number of water breaks as exercise reps. Today Brandon is far better than he was before. But James, having gone through the process himself, understands that Brandon needs to see his improvement for him to believe that it has happened. Today's training session has all the same circuit training as Brandon's first workout, but beneath the surface, it's all loaded with self-discovery.

> James: "Okay, Brandon, great work. Grab some water while we go over some results."
>
> Brandon: (panting) "Sounds good."
>
> James: "On our first day, you did thirteen jumping jacks in our one-minute test. Today, you nearly tripled it with thirty-six. That's a huge improvement, and I'm loving where this is going. How does that feel?"
>
> Brandon: "Wow, didn't even know you were timing me."
>
> James: "That's why I'm here. I timed everything. Sometimes, we can be the last ones to recognize progress, and if you think that was good, check this out: day one on the bear crawls you did one rep forward and back. Do you remember how many you did today?"
>
> Brandon: "Seven?"

James: "Exactly. If we keep moving in this direction, I could see you hitting double digits by this time next week."

How would you feel if James was your personal trainer? By taking this approach, what happened to Brandon's chances of seeing a real change in his body image? Let's break down some essential ingredients to creating The Evidence of Muscle Memory.

1. Evidence before Compliments: Any praise without evidence will not stick. James layered in his belief for Brandon's fitness capability once he had communicated the evidence.
2. Time and Distance: Objective data is hard to argue with. Had James just shared his opinions, they would not have continued past the negative and pessimistic filter in his client's head.
3. Self-Discovery is Everything: Once Brandon was presented with the proof, he was given the chance to discover his progress. James may have "wrapped the gift" of self-discovery, but he let Brandon open it. When the professional guides the experience toward self-discovery, a client's progress can transform into something much more powerful: belief.

You don't need to use the words "muscle memory" for this to be effective—this isn't a book of magical customer service incantations—but anything you present that reflects the benefits of Muscle Memory will communicate the value of it. Keep in mind that even the bumps in the journey to product progress can elevate your standing as a professional as long as you communicate them and have a plan to get past them. Finally, Muscle Memory is the activation of value, pure and simple. Until you can play the guitar, drive the car, or hit the golf ball without apologizing to your foursome in advance, the activity will remain an idea with a diminishing return. Show me the service professional that communicates the path to muscle memory, and I'll show you someone that has plenty of clients following right behind them.

CHAPTER 5

Return on Investment

A company's slogan is a lot like reading a menu; it can give you a vivid description with inspiring detail, but the slogan can't cook the food. If your food tastes nothing like the description, or if it's served to you cold in temperature or service, then the experience is flagged as a contradiction. Company slogans are only as great as the professionals that deliver upon them. Our goal as service professionals is to ensure that the food matches its description or that our service matches our slogan. To do so consistently requires one central ingredient, our ultimate goal in our Customer Service Choreography: a Return on Investment.

"My number one goal is to make sure you see a wonderful return on your investment." Whether it was your broker or your personal trainer, hearing that would let you know that you had an ally and were working with someone that has a target that goes beyond the here and now. The purpose of this chapter isn't just to just create a list of phrases to use to "build a better menu," it's also to build an awareness of the types of investments our clients make and how to build a return that reflects that.

Any investment presents some form of risk, but it's the service and skill we provide that can change that leap of faith into an informed choice.

Before we continue, let's establish one important rule: not all investments, or their returns, are financial. You may invest time into teaching your kid how to ride a bike, but it would be a crime against parenting if you expected some type of financial return from your six-year-old. Our customers make investments that aren't always financial but are worthy of our awareness. Missing out on them would be a crime against service.

So, with that in mind, let's take a look at four types of investments to put into our choreography and determine how this chapter can give you, the service professional, a great return on your investment in the process.

THE THREE SERVICE INVESTMENTS

1. The Investment of Time: Without an awareness of this investment, things can go from pleasant to volatile in no time at all. Recognizing the value of time is as important to great service as recognizing the fuel gauge on your vehicle.
2. The Investment of Effort: When we recognize the investment of effort, we'll get a return of more effort. When we lose that recognition of effort, we'll see a diminishing return of effort.
3. The Investment of Money: While the investment of money is self-explanatory, delivering a return will always determine whether future investments will be made.

1. The Investment of Time

Time is money. You've heard that one before, I'm sure. Money can be earned, lost, and replaced. Time, on the other hand, cannot. So, if you really think about it, time isn't necessarily money, but time, most certainly, is precious. So much so that in the hierarchy of investments our customers can make, the investment of time has the most value because of its scarcity.

The Investment of Time recognizes the period where a customer is engaged with a product or service. Whether that is seen or unseen, the investment can begin, and continue, far beyond the confines of your business. The return on that investment could be as simple as a grateful acknowledgment, but any investment with a positive return is an investment a customer will continue to make.

You may not have ever met, or heard of, Alfred Levy, but he's responsible for one of the greatest business improvements of the last half century. Levy is the patent holder for telephone hold music. What began as a mistake—a wiring issue on his telephone system was picking up music from a nearby radio—resulted in a revolutionary solution. "Listening to a completely unresponsive instrument is tedious and calls often are abandoned altogether or remade which leads to annoyance and a waste of time and money," Levy wrote. So he developed the patent and being on hold changed forever.

Whether you detest it or tolerate it, we can learn a lot about the Investment of Time with hold music. Regardless of the tools your company uses for handling inbound phone calls, chat messages, or long lines in the queue, we as professionals cannot be the "unresponsive instrument" when it becomes our turn to engage.

1. Design the Scenery

Visit any theme park over summer vacation and you're likely to find hour-long lines for the popular rides, maybe even longer. While every park will compete for guests based on the thrills and excitement of their rides, the Disney parks are the gold standard for the Investment of Time. Why? Because they consider the line as part of the experience.

Consider the ride Indiana Jones Adventure: Temple of the Forbidden Eye. Rather than a standard serpentine-type line, the builders, better known as Imagineers, placed elements of the Indiana Jones movies throughout the line experience. This includes everything from a tropical jungle landscape, caves, passageways, and even a few booby traps. The ride itself is a storyline separate from any of the Indiana Jones movies, which adds to the overall experience and, in effect, reduces any of the natural frustration associated with a long wait.

Long lines are a given, but Disney's approach to reducing the frustration of long lines is nothing short of brilliant. Every subtle clue, from the petroglyphs on the wall to the vintage details in the decor, is an acknowledgment to every guest who has invested their time.

So how can you design the scenery in your business? As exciting as it might be to add a jungle landscape to your waiting room and hand out decoder cards for the petroglyph messages painted on the walls, there are some alternatives that won't require a Disney budget or dozens of Imagineers.

- Acknowledge: If a customer has been waiting for any period of time, it's critical that we acknowledge that wait time. Something as simple as, "Thank you so much for your patience" or "I know how long you've been looking forward to this" can keep the time invested accounted for. An acknowledgment in itself is a return on their investment.

- Project: Sometimes it's not the people waiting "on hold" but it's their goals that are stuck in a holding pattern. The ability to project a Return on Investment accounts for the goals that they have and a strategy that leads to their desired result. While not every goal will be something you can deliver at face value, every goal deserves your effort, interpretation, and strategy.

  "Based on your goals, I believe that this strategy is going to lead to the best return on your investment."

- Effort: Any Investment of Time deserves an effort on the customer's behalf. This is the tradeoff. Whether this comes in the form of a simple smile, opening up a new kiosk for faster service, or exceeding the clients' expectations with a credit to their account, if time has been invested, then our effort should be its dividends.

2. Assume the Invisible

At some point, you've probably seen it. That image of the huge iceberg with the top 10 percent of it showing, compared to the bottom 90 percent submerged beneath the water. It's commonly used as a proverb for "there is more to the story than what you see." A ship captain wouldn't need the full dimensions of said iceberg before making adjustments to the ship's path. He can assume what he can't see.

In the Investment of Time, the consumer has spent a far greater amount of time considering the product, your business, and your digital content before you've ever interacted with them. Translation: There's a lot more to their "iceberg" than you may see on the surface. Accounting for that time and assuming the invisible helps you to navigate your service accordingly. Here's an example:

One of our standard questions with our new dance students is, "How long have you been thinking about taking dance lessons?" There are two vastly different responses we'd typically get. The first is best described as the last-minute shopper: "I don't know. I just drove by and decided to try it out." The second shares their Backstory: "I've been thinking about doing this for the last twelve years." Based on the information, we have one iceberg that is much clearer to see than the other. But we understand that not everyone feels comfortable sharing their history right away. Therefore, we assume the invisible and chalk up the last-minute shopper as someone who doesn't feel comfortable with us yet.

With the Backstory type, we can be more precise; with the last-minute type, we know more work needs to be done. In both cases, we operate under the premise that there is much more for us to learn. Doing so keeps us vigilant in our quest to connect and create meaningful service.

It saves time because we don't stop our momentum based on surface-level information.

Challenges to the Investment of Time

Any time you're attempting to create change you can expect some friction. In the following section, we'll explore some of the dangers to look out for as you're creating momentum in this area.

1. Wrong Customization: When the fabric of great service begins to fray, it's often because the service is tailored to the professional's comfort zone instead of a return on investment for the consumer. Whether that comes in the form of selective service, personal filters, or poor effort, at its core is an experience customized for the wrong person. If John F. Kennedy were an HR manager he might have said, "Ask not what your customer can do for you, but what you can do for your customer." Recalibrating our focus toward the customer's return is like realizing you've been looking through a telescope from the wrong end.

2. The Quantity over Quality Trap: A high volume of activity can easily rationalize a bare-minimum approach when it comes to service. After all, extra service can feel like extra time, and when there's a long line forming, or calls stacking up in the queue, it's easy to fall into the quantity-over-quality trap. But the late Tony Hsieh said it best: "We receive thousands of phone calls and e-mails every day, and we view each one as an opportunity to build the Zappos brand into being about the very best customer service. Our philosophy has been that most of the money we might ordinarily have spent on advertising should be invested in customer service, so that our customers will do the marketing for us through word of mouth."

If how you interact with your customers is the return on their time investment, then choose quality. If you know that they are your future ambassadors, then choose quality.

2. The Investment of Effort

You're next up. Your pulse is thumping harder than the beats of a rave DJ. Fortunately, your doctor is nowhere in sight, and your friends are incredibly supportive, not to mention persuasive. You fight the urge to say "dead man walking" as you walk to the handlers toward the front. You can feel the stares of your coworkers behind you—part support, part security detail—ensuring that you follow through with your obligation. If only you'd known how important karaoke was to your work group earlier. Nevertheless, you take the microphone and begin to sing your favorite 1980s rock tune. It's rocky at first—singing past your nerves is like gargling peanut butter—but by the chorus, you hit your stride. The nerve-riddled opening feels like a distant memory and, by the end of the song, you're feeling like an encore wouldn't kill you. But when your attention drifts back over to your coworkers, you realize how wrong you were. There, in the corner, the people you'll see Monday morning, the same ones that dragged you here and encouraged you to sing, are carrying on with their lives as if nothing has happened. You step closer, but there is zero recognition.

It feels like an elaborate ruse. Judging by the icy response, you really wish it were. But what this is, in reality, is a gamble that has gone wrong. When the investment of effort is there but goes unsupported, it's a gamble we will rarely make again. Effort is a transaction that we hope has an even exchange rate. All we ask for in return is some effort to acknowledge it.

How to Recognize the Investment of Effort

"Cigarette Lesson." Picture an ostentatious, beret-wearing, cigarette-wielding, director's-chair-sitting teacher of sorts. The caricature of a once-shining star that has faded, died, and been reborn as a black hole of criticism, absorbing the brightness of optimistic new talents, and giving "constructive criticism" from a distance, the only filter being the one on the cigarette. That is the antithesis of our teaching approach at Arthur Murray, but until we establish the darkest parts of the teaching universe, we won't appreciate the brightness.

The Cigarette Lesson teacher does not provide a single dividend on the Investment of Effort. They withhold praise until praise is earned. The scale is binary—it's either disappointing or it's heavenly—but the student giving the effort would be hard-pressed to survive the former to experience the latter. We've probably all experienced some type of coach, boss, or teacher that doled out praise like the final drops of water from a dusty canteen in the desert, but effort is not the unquenchable thirst this teacher thinks it is.

Recognizing effort is as important to service as recognizing a non-swimmer is to being a lifeguard. We, as customer service professionals, are the lifeguards in our industry. Our customers are the non-swimmers, and when they arrive in our business, they are in the middle of the pool. Their effort must be recognized or we will lose them. Here's what to look for:

1. Comfort Zone Alarms: Everyone has some sort of proximity alarm when venturing far outside of their comfort zone. Maybe it's a big groan, shaky hands, or a sudden shift into clipped conversation. These are just a few examples you can respond to, or anticipate, when it comes to recognizing the investment of effort. Keep in mind, as the professional, your product and work environment may be second nature to you but not to your clients.

2. Their Backstory: As mentioned in the earlier chapter, The Backstory contains all the most vital information that is relative to your client and their interest in what you offer. The better you know their story, the better you can recognize and appreciate the full breadth of the effort they put in.

3. The Feeling of Flatlining: There's a point in the learning process where progress goes from big spikes of improvement to something less visible to the amateur eye. To your client, it can feel like zero progress is being made (a progress flatline). A great professional, on the other hand, is a progress detective; they can find it on a granular level. Even if the progress hasn't reached its zenith, it's the high-touch service experts that can point out one incremental step of improvement along the way.

4. (What Looks Like) Zero Effort: From time to time, a client may completely detach from the experience. What can come across as zero effort is an opportunity to acknowledge the investment of effort that is in front of them. As the professional, err on the side of communicating belief: "I know this is outside of your comfort zone, but I'm here to support you, and with your help, I think this could deliver a great return on investment. Are you ready to give it a shot?"

5. Obvious Difficulty: As the navigator on the buyer's journey, areas of difficulty have the benefit of being obvious but the challenge of, well, being challenging. Fortunately, your client won't be going it alone in the process. Their return is a steady dialogue of encouragement, like a husband repeating "you're doing great" to his wife in labor. Steady, optimistic feedback can cut through the challenge.

One of my favorite stories on the Investment of Effort happened when I was in the ninth grade. I went from a private K–12 school where I knew and grew up with everyone to a public high school where I knew two people. My freshman year class alone was more than double the size of the school I left, but I was excited to venture out and explore the opportunities of a real high school with all the major sports, with no school uniforms, and with school dances. My only experience with school dances had come in the form of movies I'd watched growing up. In fact, at times, in my K–12 school, I felt a little like Kevin Bacon in

Footloose. I had this growing interest in dancing, but it wasn't allowed at our school. So, safe to say, I was excited about the first school dance my freshman year.

A guy I had met in my homeroom class asked, "Hey, you going to the dance Friday?"

Reflexively, wanting to fit in, I blurted out, "Yeah, are you?"

He said he was going and told me he'd meet me there. Not only was this going to be my first dance, but it felt like I was getting some new friends thrown into the deal. I appealed to my mom, and she allowed me to use my entire school year shopping budget on a single Nike tracksuit—black, white, and bright neon green—to match my new sneakers. It was the most expensive outfit I'd ever owned.

I couldn't wait for that Friday to arrive. I had images in my mind of the high school dances in films like *The Karate Kid* and *Can't Buy Me Love.* When the evening rolled around, my mom and stepdad drove me to the dance, and then something struck me in the drop-off lane in the parking lot—where was I going to meet the guy? Speaking of the guy, was his name Brandon? He was my only lifeline for this bold new world I was stepping into, and I hadn't thought to set a firm meeting spot. So I did what any future dance professional would do; I asked my mom if she'd walk with me to the entrance.

This is where my mom, a master-level music teacher and business owner, demonstrated how important it is to recognize the Investment of Effort.

We walked toward the sounds of thumping bass music emanating from the school cafeteria. From a distance, you'd have seen a lanky kid in black, white, and bright neon walking with the speed of a minesweeper and his mother dutifully matching his pace. I remember scanning the quad for signs of my nameless friend; nothing. I couldn't spot him, but some other students spotted me. Some seniors—I'm assuming they were because of their size and facial hair—locked in on the scene in front of them: a freshman and his mom. If reinforcing the social hierarchy on campus was their full-time job, I was making things incredibly easy for them.

"Hey, momma's boy! What's the matter?" they called out. The full social impact of showing up with my mom hit me like a water balloon to the face. I took evasive action. I averted my eyes from the senior welcoming committee and quickly communicated my split-second response to my mother to account for this social threat. "Mom," I whispered through the side of my mouth, "quick, act like you're my teacher."

Without a question or delay, she sat me down on a bench in the school quad and conducted an impromptu teacher-student conference. "You know, Christopher, I'd like to discuss some of those missing English assignments." She said it as if she'd been teaching there for years and as if these kinds of conferences always took place within fifty feet of school dances. I nodded my head, doing my best to play my part in the scene, and hoping that it would somehow take the seniors off of my scent. It didn't work.

"Aww, his mom is his date for the dance," they called out. It felt like the eyes of one hundred people looking at me. My mother continued, speaking to me as my English teacher, and projecting her voice a bit louder to really sell the masquerade. She put her hand on my back and gave me the look of "no matter what, it's going to be okay." Then, taking a page out of my favorite movies, I stood up, thanked my English teacher for her help, and walked right past the jeering seniors. There were no heroic karate kicks, and there wasn't a group of my ninth-grade classmates cheering me on, just my mom watching her black, white, and neon-clad son taking a giant leap toward a dance career.

My mother is not a dancer, but as a music teacher, she's seen her fair share of music students overcome by the fear of performing. She's done everything from priming every student on how to be a great audience from day one to joining kids on the piano bench to assisting them through times where they need the most help. She understands all the signs of effort, she knows all too well the debilitating effects of Comfort

Zone Alarms, and she possesses the skill of support and the vital role it plays in building confidence.

She witnessed me encountering the most difficult scenario in my new high school life and gave me enough support to get me past the bullies and through the door.

I never did find my friend that invited me to the dance, but in the grand design of things, I wouldn't have done things any different. That moment has always been the empathy anchor for understanding how our dance students can feel and the special bond that can form with someone that helps you through it.

Keys to Implementation:

- Waiting for someone to "earn" encouragement is a recipe for losing a client.
- Support, both verbal and non-verbal, is essential for delivering a return on the Investment of Effort.
- Know the warning signs of Comfort Zone Alarms—change in body language, tone of voice, and the like.
- Just because your client can't see or feel progress doesn't mean they aren't making any. Use your professional-level insights to pinpoint where they are in the process.
- Recognizing effort is the key to future investments in effort.

3. Investment of Money

Ben Franklin once said, "An investment in knowledge pays the best interest." To which I'll add that, oftentimes, the dividends of knowledge come from a series of poor decisions. When my job as a dance teacher included the conversation of money, I became as elusive as a guy who owed money to the mafia. I could talk about anything with my students, but the money they were investing just seemed to make me squirm. It's embarrassing to think about today, but that investment in knowledge—backed by those poor decisions—is what has led to this chapter.

You don't need to be a financial planner to use the phrase "return on investment." If I could re-write my customer service history, that would be the message I'd share with my younger self. Everyone wants to hear that you are interested in helping them benefit from their financial commitment. Whether you're a welder or wedding cake baker, what is the expected return on the investment? The moment you share that, you're in an elite class of customer service professionals.

Not to mention, communicating that reduces the natural worry that can set in when your logical brain gets the memo from your emotional brain on the transaction.

Since a financial investment is much easier to measure than things like effort, for example, it's important that we account for it and communicate it without hesitation. So let's explore some ways to acclimate ourselves to this area of what we do and discover some key takeaways to implementing this in your Customer Service Choreography.

Six Rules for the Investment of Money

1. Acknowledge: Being a service professional means that you get paid for your work. Even nonprofit charities will thank you openly for your contribution. So why should we be any different? Being open and thankful about a purchase may seem like basic customer service survival, like smiling, but we all know that even the most basic things can degrade if we aren't actively working on them. In some cases, your customers may be paying a monthly subscription for their service. If all they receive is a monthly invoice, are they really getting a renewed perspective on the Return on Investment? Probably not. A receipt is a printout of what the service might cost, but communicating the Return on Investment is what will reveal its value.

2. Use the Phrase "Return on Investment": You'd want your financial planner to use that phrase in every meeting, right? Do the same for your product after a purchase: "My number one goal is

to ensure that you get a great return on your investment." Even if your product is skill-based, like personal training, thanking them for their trust and explaining your commitment to helping them see a Return on Investment will ensure that future investments are made.

3. Strategize to Maximize Returns: Every financial commitment should be an opportunity to renew, or affirm, the strategy with your customer. No one wants to make a bigger commitment only to find out that it has a "same old, same old" strategy. So ask yourself, what can you suggest to help them maximize that return and even accelerate their growth? For example: "Thank you for trusting us with this new upgrade to our enterprise-level service. My number one goal is to show you a great return on investment, so let's talk strategy. This new upgrade includes a full-service onboarding team that will give you and your employees a faster turnaround time to add our features to your platform." Without that interaction, regardless of what may be listed on the quote sheet, it can feel like, "You're now paying extra money for the same experience. Thanks." Bottom line, treat every investment as your opportunity to communicate, or amplify, the vision.

4. Course Correct: At some point, your client might hit a rough patch with the product or the service. Use Return on Investment as the North Star that you use to recalibrate if things get knocked off track: "The last thing I'd want is for this mix-up to stand in the way of you seeing a great Return on Investment, so I'm going to put together a solution to make sure that doesn't happen again." In a marriage, you aren't solving problems to "survive another week together," it's for a bigger objective that goes beyond the moment "to love each other, 'til death do us part." When you're presented with challenges, "continuing to be our client" is basic survival, "delivering a return on investment" has a higher

ceiling and speaks on behalf of the client's goals and not just your company's.

5. Ask about Returns: "What is one thing that you can think of that would make you feel like this was a great investment for you?" You and your client could have two completely different interpretations of what will truly be a great return on their investment. You may have some ideas, your client may have expressed some already, but sometimes those are harder to articulate earlier in the process. It never hurts to maintain dialogue with your clients about what their immediate or long-term vision is for your product. This continues to customize the experience to your customer and solidifies your collaborative expertise.

6. Create, Celebrate, and Set Future Milestones: As the professional, you can use the tools laid out in the Muscle Memory chapter to create milestones: "We'll know we're on the path to a great return on investment when we've completed this lesson in a week's time." Maybe the client finally nailed a new chord in their guitar lessons or completed their fifth year enjoying your company's product. Whatever it is, be prepared to spot it. The last thing you'd want is for your customer to be the one reminding you of their important milestones. Lead the way by spotting them, communicating them to your client, and celebrating. It doesn't have to be anything extravagant, but simple congratulations or a card can go a long way. Feel free to take it further if you'd like, but in a business environment where these things are often overlooked, taking the time to show you are paying attention will mean a lot. Finally, any current achievement creates the permission to talk about the next one. (The only exception, and I'm speaking from experience here, is if your achievement is the birth of a child. Under no circumstances should you set the agenda for the next baby in the delivery room.) All kidding and childbirth aside, each step forward in their progress warrants setting some new milestones.

PUTTING IT ALL TOGETHER

Author Robertson Davies once said, "The eye sees only what the mind is prepared to comprehend." If we only see what we are prepared to see, hopefully this chapter has helped you to comprehend the opportunity when we incorporate a Return on Investment into your Service Choreography. It is the big picture result, the North Star, and it can be measured and communicated by far more than money.

CHAPTER 6

Let the Choreography Begin

This is probably as good a time as any to share The Backstory on where this choreography came from. It was the spring of 2008, and Daisey and I had just taken the biggest risk in our business life since becoming business partners in 2003: We opened our second location. Arthur Murray Livermore was the first brand new location in Northern California in over two decades, and with the support of our students, staff, and with Arthur Murray Hayward being one of the top ten locations in the world for a third consecutive year, we felt like the time was right.

In our time working in the same school together, Daisey and I had encountered and overcome so many challenges that we felt like an unstoppable dynamic duo together. We could create great momentum in the school together, but our goal was to create something bigger. We wanted to replicate the magic of our first location and turn it into a legacy in future ones. So we made the tough decision: Daisey would cover the Hayward location, and I'd be twenty minutes away at the new location in Livermore.

Parents understand the seismic shift between having a single child and adding a second to the household, and this was no different. We had no idea at the time that our second "baby" would actually be a set of twins.

We received a phone call from Wayne Smith, head of franchisee relations at our company headquarters. He was coming into town and wanted to set up some time to meet. It turned out that Arthur Murray Redwood City was going to be shut down. The staff had walked out, the owner had one foot out the door, and corporate wanted to see if we'd be interested in taking on another studio. So, after several conversations and a lunch date with Mr. Smith, Daisey agreed and, just like that, we went from one location to three locations. Parents with two kids are equally matched (at least on paper), but parents of three are officially outnumbered.

So, with a brand-new location, and a second location in need of some serious help, we were presented with the challenge—and the chance—of creating a more systematic approach to our training. Author Michael J. Gelb once said, "You can increase your problem-solving skills by honing your question-asking ability." The questions we were honing were as follows: "How the heck are we going to do this?"—a pretty normal opening question considering the circumstances. "What is it that we do in Hayward that we can replicate in the other two locations?" This was after a few months and the dust had somewhat settled. And finally, after many long commutes in both physical and mental traffic, the question that acted as the catalyst to this book, "How can I get the staff in all three locations to communicate with the same amount of clarity?"

You see, when you peel back the layers to our secret *Avatar* world, where instead of giant blue people you have ballroom dancers sometimes covered in glitter and spray tans, we have to motivate, encourage, remind, and present ideas to our clients just like in any other industry. We had no problem training our teachers in their dancing and teaching, but where the skills varied the most was in the area where we lacked a uniform approach: communication.

Then, on my drive to Redwood City, a better question bubbled up to the surface: "If our desired result is the target, then what is our ammunition?" I kept having this image of a revolver with bullets strewn over the floor. An expert marksman can't do anything without a loaded weapon. Explaining the target in more detail or polishing the weapon won't do anything to fix an ammo problem. "Can we make the ammunition repeatable?" I wondered. All we had focused on in our training were things about the delivery (the polish) or things about the goal (the target), but we never had anything consistent about the content (the ammo).

When I arrived in Redwood City, we put it to the test. Right away, the staff all began to sound like top-notch professionals. It was like one of those shows where a home makeover reveals that there had always been a beautiful hardwood floor underneath some old carpeting; the training revealed their true potential. With the success they experienced, they developed an insatiable appetite for training and application. Within two years, the studio that nearly closed down became the number one location in the world.

Our ammo, better known today as Customer Service Choreography, revolved around five key ingredients: The Backstory, The Secret Mission, The Negative, Muscle Memory, and Return on Investment.

Think of choreography as chemistry: It will take more than one element for us to create a better reaction. So in this section we're going to create some great customer service reactions using the elements you've learned so far:

The Secret Mission:
Competitive advantage, the strategic upgrade

The Negative:
The cautionary tale

The Backstory:
The purpose, their primary reason

Muscle Memory:
Short-term milestones, improving urgency

Return on Investment:
Communicating value, big picture shared goal

To help guide you, we'll start with a relatable service situation, and then we'll add the choreography to get a feel for its practical application. Remember, you've got all the moves already, but they magnify in their power when combined together.

SCHEDULING APPOINTMENTS: CREATING PURPOSE AND URGENCY

"See you next week." You'd never know it, but those might very well be the final four words in someone's hobby. Why? Because in any service where an appointment is made, the urgency we use as customer service professionals could very well be the primary reason why that person does or does not show up. "See you next week" is a statement, slathered and slow cooked in the status quo. It's the opposite of urgent and, as a result, it fails to deliver consistent results. If the overall success of your client is directly linked to the frequency of their appointments, then it is your professional duty to present that information with purpose and clarity.

The Scenario:

You are a piano teacher and your new client, Steve, just finished the paperwork for twenty piano lessons. He's a busy professional who recently purchased a piano and has always wanted to be a musician. Typically, your clients are a lot younger, have parents who force them to practice, and they usually come in once a week after school. But Steve is clearly an adult, motivated to make up for lost time, and wants to excel at this long-awaited activity.

Combination #1: Muscle Memory + Return on Investment

> You: "Steve, I love how motivated you are to learn the piano, so here's my plan. We have to sprint right out of the gate to build up muscle memory. When we can get through these basic exercises without looking down, you're going to be well on your way to a great return on your investment. How does that sound?"
>
> Steve: "Sounds great!"
>
> You: " Excellent. I'm going to lay out a schedule that will get us there as quickly as possible."

Summary:

Aside from the fact that you can use both Muscle Memory and Return on Investment in the presentation, did you notice how confident and clear the plan sounded? Often times, a customer service professional will have a motivated student, see that as a positive, but will opt for a conservative approach to the schedule for fear of ruffling the feathers of a great client. In dancing, the leader that moves tentatively and worries about stepping on their partner's foot will step on their foot. The leader that moves decisively and with confidence will move their partner out of harm's way. It's no different with service. Err on the side of confident belief and a client will never fault you for it.

For any new activity, we need to establish the Muscle Memory quickly, so the investment of time, money, or effort isn't second-guessed, suspended, or compromised altogether. Remember, Muscle Memory is a milestone and isn't restricted to activities that require agility. It represents the point where the client and the product have become acclimated.

As a quick reminder, Return on Investment isn't restricted to the world of finance. It acts as the North Star that directs the focus of any strategy toward a bigger goal. While the conservative service rep may be focused on the week-to-week micro-goals, high-level professionals will use a big-picture macro-goal to direct the execution.

Combination #2: The Backstory + The Negative + Muscle Memory

Let's take another look at this same scenario but with slightly different choreography. This time, we'll use The Backstory, The Negative, and Muscle Memory. As a refresher, The Backstory is their purpose for seeking your product. The Negative is a cautionary tale that uses phrases like "I would hate" or "the last thing I would want" to help share a definitive strategy that steers clear of that direction. Muscle Memory is a milestone where the client has a natural use of your product or some aspect of it. Let's see how this gets Steve, the piano student, off to a great start with his new hobby.

> You: "Steve, you've wanted to play the piano for so long, and the fact that you even bought a piano tells me how motivated you are."

> Steve: "Thanks!"

> You: "Now, the last thing I'd want is for our strategy to be the problem. So here's what I'm thinking: let's set up three visits this week to really build out your Muscle Memory and get you playing your piano sooner rather than later. What do you think?"

Summary:

If you were Steve, how would this approach make you feel? Notice that the teacher didn't open with, "I want you to come in three times a week." It was only after The Backstory and The Negative were laid out. This is by design. The last thing you want as a service-minded professional is to come across as self-serving in your delivery. Instead, The Backstory and The Negative keep the emphasis on the client and their goals. The frequency of the appointments is your prescription based on those goals, and Muscle Memory is the first evidence of progress.

Combination #3: The Client is Busy

We've focused on a very motivated, almost ideal version of our piano student, Steve. So what happens when he isn't so overtly motivated? Remember, when we are venturing into the great void outside of our comfort zones, it's easy to lose our way. Even if that means choosing the comfort of a busy schedule over something rewarding.

The Solution

We're going to separate out the comfort-based logistics by acknowledging the time concern. Then we will utilize The Backstory to refresh the purpose of the original decision, add in The Negative to clarify the path we want to avoid, and create a new option.

> Steve: "You know, I've got a bunch of stuff going on at work. I probably need to think this over and get back to you."
>
> You: "I totally get it. This is a brand-new idea, and you sound like a busy guy. I know you've been wanting to learn the piano for a long time, though, and I'd hate to let this idea not work out because of it. How about we

do this, let's hold an appointment for you Friday at this same time. You can check your schedule and at the very least, we can work from there. Sound good?"

Steve: "That works."

Recap

Whether Steve is truly busy or just feeling a little anxious about taking the next step doesn't matter. What's important is that we acknowledge the concern without chasing after it. Questions like "Well, what are you doing?" or suggestions like "Can't you get some time off?" don't steer the conversation to a productive place. Acknowledging the concern (without chasing) accomplishes two things: 1. It reduces any pressure the client may be feeling about their indecision about the next steps. 2. It allows you, the professional, to amplify the purpose via The Backstory without the logistics concern getting in the way.

So far, we've seen how The Negative can clarify the best path. We've seen how Muscle Memory can work as a value-building milestone and Return on Investment can act as a North Star as we guide our client to a great result. And finally, if Return on Investment is a target, then The Backstory is the pull back on an archer's bow. It's not always easy to achieve, but it possesses the greatest amount of potential energy and builds the greatest accuracy in hitting your target. But we also have another arrow in the Customer Service quiver: The Secret Mission.

Think of the Secret Mission as the customer service equivalent of an exclusive tip. Whether that's the best study strategy to pass the BAR exam or the best smoked old fashioned suggested by your bartender, people love a great recommendation. Here's an example of how that could apply in our Steve-the-piano-student scenario.

Combination #4: The Secret Mission

> You: "Steve, we've had a lot of students over the years that had all the right goals but let their busy schedule stop them from making noticeable progress. That's not going to be us. What we're going to do is condense your learning to speed through the initial learning stage. How does that sound?"

Recap

The Secret Mission is a great way of making a recommendation or course correcting a choice that won't lead to the results that they want. Remember, silence is agreement, and the professional that is silent through a suboptimal plan is endorsing it. To add impact to your version of The Secret Mission, here are some keys to keep in mind:

1. Create Contrast: Share the common option to highlight your Secret Mission.
2. Plural First: Keep any average choices plural to avoid sounding unprofessional.
3. Not Us: Enlist your client in your strategy.
4. The Plan: Lay out the details of what you will do. This is your hot tip, your inside scoop, your Secret Mission.

But, as is the case with all of our Customer Service Choreography basics, these are movable pieces that should be tailored to fit the conversation. Let's explore how the Secret Mission can pair well with Muscle Memory.

Combination #5: The Secret Mission + Muscle Memory

> You: "Steve, now that we have your lessons enrolled, I want to talk strategy. Sound good?"

Steve: "Definitely."

You: "We have a lot of students who have all the motivation but start to lose momentum because of their strategy. That's not going to be us. We're going to double up on your appointments to build your muscle memory as quickly as possible. How does that sound?"

Steve: "Sounds incredible. Let's do it."

However you decide to pair the components together, the goal is to keep you and your team sounding confident and prepared in a customer conversation. All throughout 2008, I worked on this with our teams. I'd visit one of our locations, load up some customer scenarios, add the components, and we'd do the conversational equivalent of circuit training. "Okay, guys, this time let's work on scheduling an appointment for a new student using The Backstory and Muscle Memory." With three different business locations, but with the same training toolkit, I had a built-in gauge to see how effective this new training approach was. It wasn't just effective because of its clarity and direction, it also highlighted how inefficient I had been as a trainer before that.

Think of the "hunt and peck" version of typing. Your hands can hover over the keys, you're guided through visual cues, and your typing speed and overall efficiency are egregiously low. I could always find the right training keys, but I couldn't do so with the same turnaround time as what you're reading right now. Call it Customer Service Choreography or the service training typing home row, it helped me create a consistency to my training.

As teachers, we train our dance students to be "green light dancers," meaning that they can dance to any music that is playing because they have a repertoire of dances and skills at their immediate disposal. Based on where we are in this chapter, it only seems fitting to take our Customer Service Choreography in a different direction to change up the "music" and explore how the components can combine on a different business "dance floor."

Combination #6: Muscle Memory + Return on Investment

Your new client, Jessica, just added the enterprise-level software package for her company. You are her point of contact and now in charge of bringing her up to speed on how to use it ("onboarding," in the parlance of the tech world). Despite her company being an e-commerce website, Jessica, by her own admission, is not a tech person. She's gone back and forth with you with questions about the product and has mentioned that the price was a bigger investment than she anticipated. But you understand the value of your company's software. Your company's software will streamline the ordering process for active shoppers and stay in contact with shoppers who have abandoned their shopping carts. The software is exactly what the company needs, but that's just your opinion until Jessica can learn how to use it. If she does, she'll see the value of this investment. If she doesn't, the investment could transform into something else entirely to her: An unnecessary expense.

Our Strategy

Based on what we've learned so far about Jessica, can you see some areas where certain parts of our Choreography could connect together? Let's break this down into an acronym: PSBC, or Problem, Solution, Benefit, Close.

> The Problem: Jessica is not a tech person. The learning curve could be a challenge. She can't justify the cost of the product.

The Solution: A plan to deliver Muscle Memory with the product. Accelerate the schedule so her progress outpaces buyer's remorse.

The Benefit: Return on Investment. When she can utilize the product and see how the features can help her streamline the ordering process and win back old customers, she'll see the expense as an investment.

The Close: If, Then, Love. We're going to utilize this clear three-part finish to eliminate any conversational lag time at the conclusion.

You: "Jessica, we've got the software installed, and now it's time to cover strategy. Are you ready?"

Jessica: "As ready as I'll ever be."

You: "I really want to kickstart the learning process. The sooner you can get our software into your muscle memory, the sooner you're going to see a great return on your investment. Does that sound okay to you?"

Jessica: "Definitely. I hate buying something that I can't use, so anything I can do to start using this will be great".

You: "Perfect. Here's what I'm thinking: with a little skillful scheduling, I think we can get a month's worth of training done in the next two weeks. If you're up for it, then I'd love to show you some available times we can choose."

Jessica: "Let's do it."

Recap

A benefit without a solution will just come across as a sales pitch. A solution without a problem just feels like unsolicited advice. This is why understanding the problem of your customer is essential. Think of anything you've ever bought but never used. You bought it expecting a Return on Investment. No one purchases a treadmill with the hope of it someday becoming a drying rack for your laundry, but it very well could be if there isn't a plan in place for using it. That's where Muscle Memory comes in. It is all about action. It has the capability of turning ideas into application. If Return on Investment is finishing the race, then Muscle Memory is the shorter milestones that stockpile the proof to feel like that finish line is possible.

■　■　■

In Jessica's case, there are a lot of traditional brick-and-mortar businesses that want to make an attempt to create a new digital offering, but they are stuck at the doorway facing an unknown digital abyss. Muscle Memory—and a strategy to accelerate its development—provides a solution to Jessica's problem. Finding a Return on Investment takes its place as the benefit and big picture goal. Connecting to the client by empathizing with their concerns allows you to offer support that is a service, and not something overly technical.

The Problem They Can See, the Problem You Can See

There are times when a customer will share a problem with you. It would be a shame if you ignored it, diminished it, or quickly pivoted to a solution after they shared it. This isn't to say that their problem should halt any plans you had to share a solution, it's that your job is to acknowledge that problem before offering a quick solution.

There will be times when the problem is invisible to the client. This is where your professional perspective will help the customer acknowledge, and hopefully not diminish, the potential problem you want them to avoid. Whether it's a problem they can see or a problem you can see, using The Negative helps to solve both challenges. Think of The Negative as your multi-purpose problem tool. Here's an example:

When we were new parents, any lack of sleep was always an easy tradeoff for the wonderful moments with our kids. Whether it was bedtime, bath time, or exploring the neighborhood, everything seemed to be an adventure. That is, of course, until I'd come face-to-face with the villain in our early parenting story: the shot lady. I didn't know her real name, but I did know that after a few of our visits with the pediatrician, she'd be waiting for us, needle in hand. She was my parenting enemy.

On one visit, my son had three standard vaccination shots scheduled, and just as she was preparing the first, I stopped her. "Stop. Please," I said. "How can you do this?" It blurted out on some subconscious, family protector level of my brain.

The shot lady paused, looked at me, and said, "I know it's tough." Her voice was reassuring. "But I can do this because I know what problems these help your son avoid." She motioned to the syringes. "We could just do one of them, but then that would mean you'd be coming back for two extra visits just to see me for the others. Is that what you want?" she asked. Realization washed over me. The shots may have felt like a problem, but they were actually the solution to a larger one.

That day, the shot lady taught me a valuable lesson with her perspective, and I also learned that she wasn't a heartless villain in my early life as a parent. She helped me zoom out from my problem to see the full picture. That conversation became my regular reminder, my shot mantra if you will, for any future trips to see her. Whether it's a problem they can see or one only you can see, as a professional, you possess a perspective that your client can, and should, benefit from.

In this next scenario, we're going to add The Negative to help add some professional perspective to our recommendation. Even if your client hasn't experienced the problem yet, anticipating it and offering a solution this way will be something they will appreciate. Also, it's fun to point out that this will be our bit of Customer Service Choreography with three components: The Negative, Muscle Memory, and Return on Investment.

Combination #7: The Negative + Muscle Memory + Return on Investment

We're going to revisit the Jessica scenario again. She wants to add a software product to improve the checkout process and stay engaged with shoppers that didn't complete their transactions, but this time, something is much different. Jessica wants to think it over. She hasn't purchased the product yet, and her concern around the learning curve is putting her ability to see the overall value of the purchase in jeopardy. Using our PSBC layout, let's look at how this will be constructed:

> Problem: This has a few parts. Jessica's first problem is the learning curve. She isn't a techie person. This leads us to her second problem: she can't justify the cost of the software because the first problem is blocking her vision for seeing the value of the purchase. Finally, the problem Jessica can't completely see is the cost of continuing with the status quo. She's losing sales that this software can help her prevent, and postponing a decision is more expensive than she realizes.

> Solution: We'll use Muscle Memory as the first part of our solution. This is our confident plan to eliminate any concern about her ability to use the product. We'll use The Negative to speak to the problem she can't see: her status quo is costing her money.

Benefit: The benefit here is Return on Investment. If Jessica makes the purchase, the software will pay for itself because of the lost sales it will help her avoid.

Close: We will utilize the "If, Then, Love" finish to keep the end of the conversation concise and sharing a clear intent.

Jessica: "You know, I think I just need to thing this over. It's a big purchase, and I just don't think I'm going to be able to use it, to be honest."

You: "I totally get it. I know this feels like a big step, but I also know that you won't be taking that step all on your own. My number one job is to help you get this software integrated as quickly as possible, and I'm going to be with you every step of the way. I'd hate to have that concern stand in the way of you seeing a great return on investment. So if you're up for it, then I'd love to get you started with a trial version of our product so you can see how well it works. What do you think?"

Jessica: "Okay. I can give that a try."

Even if the response you receive isn't the response you hoped for, zooming out to the bigger purpose is never a bad idea. Remember, your client will never have the same perspective as you do, so we can't judge them negatively if they can't see what you are capable of seeing. Instead, help them zoom out, err on the side of positive intent and perspective building, and even if they decline, at least they'll be doing so with a clearer picture.

THE CHOREOGRAPHY IS A DOUBLE-EDGED SWORD

Throughout this chapter, we've created our choreography in a variety of ways. Just like a great chef, a great dancer, or a fluent speaker; the more familiar you are with the components, the easier it is to combine them. As great as these conversational assets may be, there's a flip side to them we need to be aware of.

The doomsday scenario in any comic book is if a superhero, blessed with some type of superhuman abilities, uses their powers for evil. Your Customer Service Choreography may not be as exciting as heat vision or running faster than a speeding bullet, but it can certainly upgrade your social superpowers in a big way. Here's how we avoid using them in the wrong way. It's called "The Curse of My."

The Backstory can transform from the relevant history of your client with your product to "My Backstory." This is when a customer service professional lets their own Backstory filter their interactions with a client. This can stem from their own insecurity about the financial or time investment with the product to a general dislike for the work they do. When a professional's personal feelings stand in the way of them delivering the intended experience, they cease to act professional.

The Secret Mission revolves around an invitation to try something that defies the status quo. With "The Curse of My," that invitation is withheld. Customer Service employees that are thinking more about their feelings than the customer experience will share obligations and skip sharing opportunities.

The Negative lays out a cautionary tale to highlight the path that will deliver the best value. Customer Service staff that suffer from "The Curse of My" would see The Negative as the name implies: a negative. In doing so, they'd stay silent when it came to making a course correcting recommendation. Instead, they'd rely on the hope that the client would figure it out on their own.

"The Curse of My" can take Return on Investment and repurpose it into the transactional phrase of "what's *my* return on investment?" When a customer service professional approaches their work with a singular, monetary motivation, they are incapable of forming a sincere connection with the client.

SUCCEEDING WITH CUSTOMER SERVICE CHOREOGRAPHY

So, right out of the gate, let's remember not to use the training for evil. All kidding aside, keep in mind that our five components are there to add structure to your service interactions. These components aren't magic words, and you won't get extra agreement points with your clients if you use them all in one breath. The goal is to create a confident and consistent way to connect to your customer.

Finally, let's talk about measuring your results. There's a slim-to-none chance that someone leaves an online review for your business saying, "I never thought a customer service professional would share my Backstory so eloquently, and the fact they mentioned a return on investment really impressed me." The interesting thing about customer service is that it's easier to appreciate than it is to pinpoint. Your customers may not be able to articulate exactly what it is that makes you easy to interact with, but they'll probably generalize it with phrases like, "they're so easy to talk to," "I really feel comfortable when I'm there," and "they treat me like I'm part of their family."

Any production requires a lot of practice behind the scenes to ensure that the final show is a success. They won't need to know all the hard work you've done to appreciate how easy it is to do business with you.

CHAPTER 7

Adding a Frame

Truth be told, I never cut any classes in high school. I was, however, incredibly late for one, so much so that my teacher gave me a stern warning. So, what does this have to do with customer service? I would have been on time had I been better at getting to my point, not beating around the bush, and landing the proverbial plane. In this chapter, we're going to do that by adding what we'll call a Conversational Frame.

You see, as much as I love customer service and communication skills now, back in high school was another story. I wasn't necessarily shy—I had a lot of friends—but when it came to talking to girls, my brain seemed to veto any attempt I made to converse confidently. The day of my nearly-cut class was the day I asked a girl I liked to be my date for the winter formal. What began as an attempt at the end of our lunch period extended well into my fifth-period journalism class.

Instead of just asking her if she would be my date for the winter ball, I decided to "warm up" to the question by engaging in small talk: "That party last week was pretty cool," and "Can you believe that he got that brand new car?" Pathetic, I know. Then, when it came time to do the asking, the direct question was replaced with qualifiers: "sort of," "kind of," "maybe," and other things like that. My pitch went from a sixty-second question to a thirty-minute master class in beating around the bush. Eventually, maybe to put me out of my misery or just to get to class, she asked, "Are you asking me to the winter ball?"

There was a pang of embarrassment, followed by a sputter and some nervous laughter, and then I said, "Well, yeah." She looked relieved, which made me think I must have completely weirded her out, but then—she accepted. She ran to class, I did the same, and the result seemed to dampen the inelegant presentation I had made.

In customer service, we can have all the positive intentions to have great communication, but the fact is that we may fall into the same trap—small talk, qualifiers, and confusion—if we don't have a framework to follow. Let's explore some examples of how to add a conversational dance frame, so we can speak with confidence, clarity, and keep things concise while we're at it.

THE SOONER, THE SOONER

Parents have been utilizing this conversational frame since the dawn of parenting: "The sooner you eat your dinner, the sooner you can watch a movie." One hundred years earlier, it might have been, "The sooner you eat your supper, the sooner we can read Jules Verne by the fireplace."

We can see the same framework in place on vacation with our friends: "The sooner we get checked in, the sooner we can relax by the pool." Even if it's not always under the most positive pretense ("I don't care what you choose. The sooner you pick a movie, the sooner we can start our date"), this tool has found its way into everyday conversation so frequently that you may not even realize how often you've used it. That is, until now.

The construction of this framework can be reduced to two basic principles: the work and the reward.

If we look at the phrase "the sooner you do your homework, the sooner you can play Xbox," we can see that "homework" is the work and "play Xbox" is the reward. This approach isn't just useful because of its timeless simplicity, but it also has an underlying foundation in something even more powerful: it stays positive.

If you've ever read books on leadership, negotiation, or sales, you've probably heard of the phrase "the carrot and the stick." The carrot is an incentive, something that will induce an audience toward a particular type of behavior. The stick, on the other hand, is a punishment if said behavior is not done. A great example of this comes from Alec Baldwin's character, Blake, the visiting sales executive in the movie *Glengarry Glen Ross*: "As you all know, first prize is a Cadillac Eldorado. Anyone want to see second prize? Second prize is a set of steak knives. Third prize is you're fired."

Let's take inventory here: Cadillac, carrot. Steak knives, another carrot. Fired, stick.

As dramatic (and comical) as that might seem, resorting to heavy-handed and emotional "stick waving" is a great example of what can happen when there's a customer service disconnect, which is precisely why using the work/reward framework is a much better alternative.

Let's look at how this frame can weave into our basics from the earlier chapters. We'll start by examining the type of "work" we want to get accomplished and then communicating what the benefit, or "reward," might be.

For dance lessons, music lessons, or medieval falconry lessons it could be:

> "The sooner we can set up your next appointment, the sooner we can put these new skills into your muscle memory."

The "next appointment" is the work and "muscle memory" becomes the reward. How cool is that? If we want to take that up a notch or continue the conversation later, we might say,

> "The sooner we develop your muscle memory, the sooner you're going to see a return on your investment."

In this version, we place "muscle memory" in the work slot and "return on investment" as the reward. This is a better alternative to a "carrot and stick" approach, which might sound something like, "If you practice, you'll be good, but if you don't, you'll waste all your money." Yikes.

In some cases, as a customer service professional, you have to be a motivator, the person that can see a customer's potential even before they can. In cases where you have to combat someone's fear and assist them beyond the confines of their comfort zone, you can adapt the sooner, the sooner into something even more descriptive.

Rather than using "the work" and "the reward," we can use "the work" and "the feeling." Here are some examples:

> "The sooner you try an obstacle race, the sooner you'll feel like you can conquer anything."

> "The sooner you make your reservation, the sooner you'll feel the benefits of planning a vacation early."

> "The sooner we launch our product, the sooner we'll feel like a real company."

While there may be some that just need a quick title of the reward, there will be others that may need a clearer, more descriptive picture. As with anything in the art of communication, use your best judgment.

THE SOONER, THE CLOSER

There are many important goals you can set out for your customers that are more process-oriented than instant results. Speaking too early about an end result can be discouraging and premature, like talking about marriage on a first date. This variation of our framework is designed to create urgency for the next step instead of the final step. Here are some examples:

> "The sooner we can knock out your workout goal this week, the closer we'll be to your target weight by the end of the summer."

> "The sooner we can get this paperwork done, the closer you'll be to picking out your furniture."

> "The sooner we launch this campaign, the closer you'll be to having a fully-functioning marketing team."

If the final step in a process is a marathon, think of the next step as a small segment of it. No one will sprint through an entire marathon, but they will toward a shorter destination. If your product is a process, use this framework to create the urgency to achieve your client's next measurable result.

I KNOW, AND I ALSO KNOW

From time to time, things won't go as planned. There will be misunderstandings, and even with the great customer service choreography you've learned thus far, there will be times when your clients turn you down. Whether you're seeking a great way to frame an apology or an entry point for replacing an outdated plan, this is the frame for you. "I know, and I also know" is your fixing frame. Here's how it works.

Similar to our "the sooner, the sooner" framework, this sentence has two slots that carry our message. In slot one, we will insert the status quo. This could be a concern they have, a problem they're facing, or even a decision they've made that you want to help them see from a different perspective. In the second slot, we'll insert an appeal. Whether that is using a benefit or their Backstory, your goal is to make slot two as compelling as possible. Finally, there's a pivot to action. Here's an example to get things started:

> "I know your schedule is crazy, but I also know that learning to dance is important to you, so let's explore some options to make this work."

We'll see that in slot one, the "crazy schedule" is our status quo. As you'll see in some other examples, stating this up front helps to both acknowledge any concerns and disarm them in the process. In doing so, the objection is less likely to distract or derail from the appeal you're making.

In slot two, we have "learning to dance" as our appeal. If you didn't guess it already, this is a basic form of The Backstory. A great appeal should outweigh any concerns in slot one and, in doing so, remind the client of a purpose that's bigger than the problem.

Finally, "let's explore" is our action to finish out this customer service choreography framework. There will be plenty of ways to add different kinds of action, but it's imperative that we follow one of my time-honored principles—made famous in my home and business by my wife Daisey—which states: never present a problem without offering a solution. Your action is step one of your solution.

To show you how adaptable this "I know" framework can be, here's an example from my life involving a few critical details: a double date, a long wait, and a shellfish allergy.

We met up with our longtime friends, Juan and Cari Jo, for dinner in a posh, outdoor shopping area in San Jose, California, where the designer labels are only outdone by the restaurant options. On this particular night, it seemed like all of Silicon Valley had converged there. Our first two attempts at a table for four brought back a similar response: over an hour wait.

For the sake of clarity and honest storytelling, I should include that neither of our wives would approve of us waiting that long for a table, especially when the temperature was beginning to drop. Both Juan and I were trying to assess the situation when I noticed one restaurant we hadn't been to before that didn't seem to be that busy: a sushi bar. It was a risky play, but we were short on options, and not to mention "cold," "hungry," and "patiently waiting" aren't words that generally go together.

"I'll be right back," I said, as I ran to the restaurant to explore my Hail Mary hunch.

"Fifteen minutes," said the hostess, over the thumping sounds of club music behind her. I ran back to share the news. This is the point in the story where I should point out a final critical detail: Juan has a shellfish allergy. The kind that wouldn't just give him an itchy throat or a mild rash. No, his allergy is more of the "someone call an ambulance" variety. So, sushi isn't his favorite.

With time and temperature already working against us, and with our only option being a restaurant that could kill one of my best friends, I had to make this presentation count.

"Okay, Juan," I said, "I know that you're allergic to shellfish and this might not be your favorite option, but I also know that our wives are cold and want to get some dinner, so here's the deal: the sushi place can seat us in fifteen minutes and, at the very least, you can get some teriyaki chicken while we're eating sushi. What do you say?"

Juan took a deep breath, smiled, and said, "Okay, let's do it." There was a cheer of celebration from Daisey, not just because she likes sushi, but because she loves short wait times. Cari gave Juan a sideways look, which, in the nonverbal parlance of matrimony, said, *Are you sure about this?* He gave her a reassuring look, mentioned the teriyaki idea, and before long, we were seated inside the sushi restaurant.

Maybe restaurant isn't the best word to describe what this place was. Imagine a nightclub that happened to be a sushi bar with decor that made you feel like you were in a real-life Japanese anime cartoon. There was a DJ spinning thumping club music, dim lighting, bright neon, and keeping with the theme, a jumbo screen showing Japanese anime on the wall. It was the sort of sushi place where a traditional Japanese menu item might be deep fried and served over bamboo and dry ice.

As we took in the menu options and settled in, our waitress came to greet us and give us some important news: "I'm so sorry," she said, "but our stove is broken." Maybe it was the music, but I didn't understand the message right away. "Our stove is broken," she said, louder this time, "we're only serving sushi tonight." Then, the full weight of the message hit us all at once: no teriyaki.

I turned to Juan—who looked like he was about to recite Al Pacino's famous line from *The Godfather Part III*, "Just when I thought I was out, they pull me back in"—and I leveled with him: "Hey man, I know they don't have teriyaki, but I know they have some great spicy tuna rolls that won't mess you up."

He went with the recommendation, more so because he's a good friend than because of anything I said to convince him. It was a memorable night, to say the least. Juan tried a sushi roll, didn't care for it; after we had finished our dinner, he had a second dinner later that night.

SLOT ONE: AVOID DERAILMENT

When it comes to effective customer service (and dancing), timing is everything. You often can't afford to take a hunt-and-peck approach to a recommendation. It needs precision. Had I opened the conversation with, "Hey guys, the sushi place only has a fifteen-minute wait," what do you think Juan's response would have been? "Sorry, I can't do sushi because of my allergy," he'd say, and for good reason. But remember, time and temperature were working against us, and I already understood the concern Juan had, which brings us to an important point.

Knowing your customer's problem is vital to constructing a solution. Albert Einstein once said, "Given one hour to save the world, I would spend fifty-five minutes defining the problem and five minutes finding the solution." Often, we're faced with a problem that we'll avoid and hope is fixed without our intervention. Using Einstein's model, that would be noticing the world-threatening problem, leaving it alone, and checking on it again like a college student continually opening the same empty refrigerator in search of a decent meal. Avoidance won't solve a problem, and it certainly won't work when that problem includes cold wives and long waits.

This is precisely why slot one is there in our framework. It is, in Einstein's words, "defining the problem" and putting it out there, on the proverbial table, for you, the professional, to address. As much as you may have heard that the customer is always right, that sentiment can be taken into convenient context. It doesn't give us license to avoid our customer's problems; it is simply stating that if you are in a position of service, the customer is the person in which you serve. This should undoubtedly include problem-solving if it is in their best interest moving forward, even if that means confronting a challenge.

SLOT TWO: PERSONALIZE YOUR APPEAL

In most cases, you'll utilize The Backstory in slot two. Remember from our earlier chapter, this is the portion of their history that has the most relevance to their role with your product. This is the time to use that. Whether there's a minor bump or a major impediment, this is the spot where you're reminding your stakeholder why they chose your brand and why you're the right professional to take action.

For example:

> "I know public speaking isn't your thing, but I also know
> that you hired me to create PR opportunities, and this
> conference is a big one, so here's what I'm thinking…."

We see the challenge in slot one: "public speaking."

Then we get the splash of rational cold water in slot two with a masterful use of The Backstory: "You hired me to create PR opportunities."

In other cases, you may go with the problem or challenge in slot one followed by The Negative in slot two. This is a great method for addressing an issue that requires a meaningful apology and taking full accountability for something that went awry. Here's an example:

> "I know that we missed the mark with the service you
> received, but I also know that the last thing we'd want
> is to have your last experience be your final impression
> of us moving forward, so, if you're open to it, we'd love
> to make it up to you."

In slot one, we have the problem clearly stated: "we missed the mark with the service…."

When we shift to slot two, you'll see The Negative in action with the telltale "the last thing we'd want."

Addressing the problem and taking full accountability for it will not only get the attention of your customer, but it will also demonstrate a genuine interest in serving, instead of a reflexive reaction to defend your earlier actions. I share with my staff all the time that pricking your finger isn't falling on the sword when it comes to owning up to our mistakes. Great service isn't restricted to ideal circumstances, so consider this frame a life raft when the service waters get rough.

SLOT THREE: TAKE DECISIVE ACTION

So, you've maintained the attention and constructed a sincere apology; this is not the time to be vague. The action you suggest should match the intention of your message thus far. Much has been said about the generous, and often abused, return policy at Nordstrom. Sure, there were people who would return items that Nordstrom had never sold them, or ever carried, but underneath it all is the willingness to serve—regardless of the circumstances or the weird returns they've had. A no-questions approach gave their frontline service professionals the decisiveness necessary to take swift action and put the customer's needs first.

I was in Philadelphia for a weekend speaking engagement. After unpacking, I realized (to my horror) that I was short one pair of slacks in my suitcase. With only a few hours to spare, I hopped in a cab, arrived at Nordstrom, and found a pair that would match my outfit. The only problem? They still needed to be hemmed, and I was running short on time. Since Nordstrom has a tailor on hand, I asked the sales associate, James, when the pants could be ready if I had them tailored. "Tomorrow. Probably after six," he said. He must have seen my face fall. I had bought the pants, but I had no way of picking them up, since I would be busy as the keynote speaker of the event.

"Do you offer deliveries, or do you know of a company I can call?" I asked.

James seemed to run through some options in his head, and he asked, "What time do you need them by?"

"Before 5:00 p.m.," I told him.

"Tell you what," he said, "I'll drive them out to you."

Sure enough, on his way home from work, I met James outside my hotel where he handed me a pressed pair of slacks, hemmed to perfection, and with a smile on his face. Talk about taking decisive action.

THE WHICH CLOSE

We can't talk about conversational framework without mentioning one of the all-time classics: the Which Close. It is to customer conversations what vanilla is to ice cream: intrinsic. Its construction is fairly simple. Rather than giving someone a single option ("Do you want to try our pizza?"), you give them a choice between two options ("Do you want to try our pizza, or would the chicken wings work better?"). A final "which" question like, "Which one would you like?" "Which will work best?" or "Which one are we thinking of going with?" helps to round out the frame.

"Never give someone an option between something and nothing" is what one of my business mentors, Claudia Marshall, said time and again. "Always give them the choice between something and something." As we are constructing the tools to deliver high-touch service, choreographed in a way to withstand even the most challenging of service environments, it's critical that we carry our ideas across the conversational finish line without any slip-ups. The Which Close is a great way to bring your presentation to a professional finish, even if it's your first day on the job or you're presenting an offer that will change your life forever.

It was Christmas Eve, and I made a mad dash to jewelry store after jewelry store until I found the right one. To be honest, I had no idea what I was doing. I'm not much of a jewelry person myself, and I didn't have any experience making this type of purchase. How could I? It's not like I'd asked someone to marry me before. I don't know if it was stepping into a new retail experience with zero knowledge or just the thought that I'd be proposing to Daisey—my longtime girlfriend, dance partner, and business partner—the next morning, but I was a little jittery, to say the least. But when I finally stepped into the store I'd heard so many radio commercials about, I could see that their service claims and customer testimonials were the genuine article. They immediately made me feel welcomed. Looking back, the jittery (okay, panicked) guy running into the store minutes before closing time was probably out of the first page of their employee training manual. At least, that's how it felt when they greeted me, reassured me that we could find the perfect ring, and never once made me feel like my budget was an issue.

"Out of these three options, which one can we put back?" the sales associate asked. I selected one that, for reasons that were never asked to be shared, I would eliminate from the decision-making process. "Now, out of these two, is there one that you think is the one, or should we select another one to compare against?" Every step of the process was a gentle process of elimination followed by a Which Close. This eliminated pressure and built my confidence with every adjustment that I made.

Eventually, I found the perfect ring: something that looked the part but could also pass as a timeless piece you might have passed down through generations. I knew that a small box sitting under our Christmas tree would be a little obvious, and so I decided to get a little creative to ensure that Daisey would have no idea it was coming. But one important note that will undoubtedly weigh in heavily on the drama of this story is this: Daisey had, on a few separate and unprompted occasions, casually mentioned that she was never getting married. That little detail might have also been a large part of the anxiety I was feeling and, most likely, the reason why this plan may contain notes of slapdash, whirlwind, and anxiety-riddled procrastination.

So, with that in mind, I decided to buy a small jewelry box to place the ring inside. I thought its rectangular shape would throw her off of any pretense that there may have been a ring hidden inside. But that didn't seem like enough, so I purchased a small box of cards with daily quotations you might get at the checkout stand at your favorite bookstore. This one was for teachers, and we were both teachers, so I figured I'd find a card that would be cute, inspiring, and romantic in a quirky sort of way. The card I found featured a child holding a paintbrush, looking up at a fence, with the words "anything is possible" written in painted kid scrawl. It was perfect. I taped the ring to the card and wrote, in my own semi-legible scrawl, "Daisey, will you marry me?"

I placed the card in the card box and the card box in the jewelry box. Then I wrapped the jewelry box in wrapping paper and placed the most important rectangular box of my life underneath the couch next to our Christmas tree. Before you pass that off as a little paranoid, I'd like to point out that I also crumpled up some wrapping paper to shield the rectangular box from view, just to be safe. The goal was simple: After unwrapping the regular gifts, I'd do that thing that all parents love to do on Christmas morning: "I'm not sure, but it looks like there might be one more gift back there behind the tree," I'd say. "Why don't you poke around and see if you can find something?" In my mind, I imagined sitting back in mock confusion as she pulled out the box, found the ring, and shouted, "Yes!" Then I'd revel in the ingenuity of my planning and commitment. But sometimes, the performance you have planned in your mind is nothing like the real thing.

What actually happened is that the moment we stepped into our living room, Daisey noticed the wrapping paper on the floor by the couch. "Did you leave this out?" she asked. Uh oh. She leaned down to pick up the stray paper and said, "Hey, what's this gift under here?" My heart dropped into my stomach. She then produced the rectangular package with an inquisitive look, and I did some quick thinking, which was challenging considering the lack of blood flow in my brain at the time. "Who is this for?" she asked.

"Uh, that is for my...brother," I said with all the sincerity of a petty thief. She set the box down; disaster averted. Well, for now, at least.

After we had unwrapped the presents under the tree, I asked Daisey to grab the box under the couch for my brother. She hesitated, but I encouraged her to continue: "Go ahead, it's really for you." She unwrapped the rectangular, wooden jewelry box and smiled as she examined the exterior with the glass jewel-tone inlay. She looked at me with genuine gratitude, thanked me, and set the box down. My internal alarm bells went off. "Why don't you, uh, open the box?" I said. She looked at me, surprised that there was more to it, and opened the box. Inside, she found the small box of teacher quotes. She held the smaller box in her hands, looked at the description written on the back, and set the cards back in the jewelry box, and the jewelry box on the floor.

"Thanks, babe," she said, and by this point, I'm sure my blood pressure reached an unprecedented level.

In the coolest way possible, as not to arouse any suspicion or frustration, I offered, "Why don't you try opening up that box of cards?"

She complied, pulled out the cards, and then said, "Wait, do you know that you bought these cards without the wrapper?"

Something spluttered out of my mouth to the tune of, "I think they came that way." She was still curious, so she opened the small box, removed the first card, admired it like you would if your grandma knitted you some socks you know you'll never wear, but you smile anyway. She then placed the top card back into the box, and the card box into the jewelry box, buried right next to my grand plans of a marriage proposal.

I gave it one final try. "Check the cards again, maybe toward the back?" I said, with an extra flare of my eyebrows, tilting my head toward the box she had been opening and closing. She smiled, went through the boxes, and produced the cards. This time she picked up the entire deck out of the box and I could see the wedding-ring-sized gap in the cards. This was it.

She finally flipped to the card that read "Anything is possible" and "Daisey, will you marry me?" She stared at it. I stared at her. Silence. Being that she was reading the message, I understood, but it was as if she was reading the first page of a novel. Then, almost inaudibly, there was a sound. It was faint, just a whisper: "Oh my God." She kept repeating it, and I kept trying to discern whether that "oh my God" was good or bad.

Flashes of those "I'm not getting married" moments popped into my head, but I fought them off. We had been through so much together: running a business, doing so by our bootstraps, turning it into one of the best in the world. Our dance partnership had improved, and so had our communication with each other. We were celebrating Christmas together in a condo we'd bought together, for crying out loud. But she kept repeating her whispered mantra, "Oh my God, oh my God, oh my God."

So, I decided, in that moment, that regardless of her answer, I would continue to love her. I wouldn't be the guy who tosses the ring down, who lets his ego take over and ends something because the timing or trust wasn't there. I decided to ask her, out loud, in the best way I knew how, and if she said no, I was prepared.

I looked her in the eye, and she looked up from the card she had been studying, with the ring taped to it, her eyes were filling with tears. I said, "Daisey, would you like an afternoon wedding or would an evening wedding be more convenient for you?"

She released a cry and a laugh almost simultaneously. We hugged, and I could feel the weight of the moment decompress. Eventually, she put on the ring, and we were engaged. Technically speaking, she never actually answered the big question, but the following October, she agreed to be my wife. She chose the evening wedding.

Looking back, the communicator I was in high school who struggled to ask a girl to the winter formal versus the guy who used a Which Close for a marriage proposal were two completely different people. The training I received in my career equipped me in such a way that it held up, even in the biggest presentation of my life.

While there were certainly some comedic mishaps in the gift-presentation department, one thing was very clear: I didn't need to have repetition at marriage proposals to confidently deliver a marriage proposal.

I just needed a conversational framework. I was the beneficiary of some great customer service choreography.

CHAPTER 8
Depth and Altitude

In customer service, there are bound to be times where frustration runs high and clarity runs low. When your customer reaches the tumultuous waters that can come with any pressurized interaction, it's in those moments that the truly gifted service professionals shine like a lighthouse. The tools covered in this chapter will help add depth to avoid the problems of communicating with surface-level language. We'll also take a look at altitude, which zooms out to reveal the bigger value of a seemingly simple decision.

If you had to give it a score out of one hundred, with one hundred being the perfect conclusion to a service encounter, where would you rank someone complaining about the service they were getting? Would it be a zero?

Now imagine the same scale. This time, your potential client never complains, but he exits your service radar like a thief in the night. Which of these two examples would have the higher ranking?

Feedback, good or bad, is useful information. In customer service, information is a gift—one that could easily be withheld. When that happens, the silent departures leave you speculating on the reasons why, with no information to determine the solutions for improvement.

So, with that being said, the real zero is the silent departure. A shade above that might be the dissatisfied customer that showers you with praise as they end their time with you (the business version of the "it's not you, it's me" talk). A complaint, on the other hand, is an opportunity to communicate. It's immediately an upgrade over speculation or some misguided hope because of a few compliments tacked onto their exit. So, let's call a complaint a fifty; it may not be one hundred, but it certainly beats a zero.

Before you consider this a bitter pill that I'm convinced tastes like gummy bears, let's clarify: What do doctors, therapists, and plumbers all have in common? They all are in the business of listening to your problems so they can do a great job. Your doctor wouldn't have much to go on if, while suffering from appendicitis, you suddenly told him, "You know, I'm not really hurt, I feel fine actually. Did I mention that you're wonderful?" Would a therapist feel relieved If you showed up to your first appointment, only to mention that you were "just browsing" when it was your time? In either example, the more honest and communicative the client is, the more effective the professional can be at what they do best.

So that leaves our plumber. Your downstairs toilet is on the fritz, and he's the guy who fixed it last time. Every leak you cleaned up, every time the drain clogged was an indictment on his work. You're just a few degrees from boiling when he shows up at your door and you say, "The toilet did that thing again, and after the three hundred bucks I paid you the last time, here we are again." The plumber, with a rational mind and excellent customer service skills, sees you, the client, as a fifty, not a zero.

He doesn't get defensive. He doesn't mutter under his breath or roll his eyes in an "I don't have time for this" sort of way. He nods his head as you're speaking, maintains eye contact to show he's listening, and responds, "I'm so sorry to hear that. You could have easily kept that to yourself and found another plumber, so I want to thank you for letting me know about this and giving me a chance to make it right." He speaks with a sincerity in his voice that indicates that he'd do whatever it takes to ensure that you are a longtime customer.

Hearing this, your return volley of criticism is stifled. This guy sounds accountable. Had he been defensive or dismissive, you would have known exactly what to do. But now, the boiling pot of frustration reduces down to something best described as warm relief. "If it's okay with you, I'd love to take a look at it," he says.

So you open your door a little wider, smile, and say, "Thank you, that would be great." Regardless of the issues you're having with your pipes, this plumber is clearly exceptional at his real job: customer service.

Let's take a look at the (sorry) plumbing of this response so it can become a repeatable asset in your customer service choreography.

ALIGNMENT AND BODY LANGUAGE

In competitive dancing, where you line up on the floor is more critical than the casual observer might think. The right alignment in a dance like the waltz can ensure that the strategic layout of your choreography can get from one side of the floor to the next virtually unimpeded, showcasing your best material with the proper rotation for each maneuver.

Without a great alignment, that same waltz routine can be as smooth as driving the bumper cars at the county fair.

In customer service, your alignment comes down to body language. Remember, you work in a realm that is governed by perception, so even the slightest shift in your facial expression can be read in a way that is inconsistent with your positive intentions. So how do you ensure that your internal intentions aren't stifled by the external perceptions? Here are four keys to putting your body language in great alignment when you're receiving tough feedback.

1. Refresh Your Perception: As crazy as it sounds, hearing tough feedback can feel threatening, which may sour your ability to

think clearly and put you into a feedback loop where both parties are making it harder to stay rational. Instead, remember that people who don't care about you or your business will just leave. People that do care, on the other hand, will speak up. As inelegant as it may come across at times, they are asking for help. Why do sports fans curse at the players they are watching on television? Because they care deeply, even if they might seem unhinged in the delivery.

2. Seek to Understand: In his book *The 7 Habits of Highly Effective People*, Stephen Covey states that you should "seek first to understand and then to be understood." This will convey interest on your part instead of an urgency to interrupt and defend your part in the situation. Imagine that you're a detective, interviewing a potential witness; every bit of information is vital to your case. You'd nod, lean in, even jot down notes, all for the purpose of understanding. If, on the other hand, you believed you were talking to a criminal, go back to number one.

3. Determine Your Ideal Outcome: The better you can describe your ideal outcome, the easier it will be to align yourself toward it. Do this ahead of time and understand that an ideal outcome is not a quick and insincere apology. If this were your spouse, where would that lead you? It may get you out of the conversation, but it won't get you out of the doghouse. An ideal outcome might be best looked at through the lens of the person sharing the feedback. What are they really asking for? What does it cost me to accept accountability? What would it cost me to deny that and dismiss their feedback?

4. Show Your Intentions: It's easy to talk about intentions. After all, your intentions are usually the best-case scenario and make perfect sense to you. The problem, on the other hand, is that no one else resides in the space between your ears. So, what can you do? Show your intentions. What people perceive about you—whether that's your body language, tone of voice, or your choice

of words—is the law, according to them. Their perception of you can be categorized as an odor or a scent. Rolling your eyes, sighing heavily, or looking distracted only adds to the odor. Nodding your head, without any defensive body language, and responding with kindness will add to the scent.

CREATING DEPTH

The phrase "you could have easily" is used to help create perspective. Sharing what the easy outcome could have been helps to highlight the outcome they've chosen. It's an acknowledgment of the effort they've made, even if that effort is being delivered in the form of tough feedback, a challenging event, or a situation in which their comfort zone is sounding its proximity alarm. The easy outcome becomes the bottom end on a scale of effort; the choice they've made, however, now sits on the top end. The result is the creation of depth, which can turn a surface-level situation into something with greater meaning.

For example:

> "You could have easily decided to go with a different person for the job, but you didn't...so I want to thank you for giving me this opportunity."

> "You could have easily kept this frustration to yourself, but you didn't.... Thank you for sharing this with me and giving me an opportunity to make things right."

> "You could have easily stayed home today and stuck with what was comfortable, but you didn't...so thank you for being here today."

A Statement of Gratitude

A skilled customer service professional understands the importance of thanking someone when they have a complaint. The goal here is to do so after you've established the depth to highlight their choice to share that concern or step outside of their comfort zone. Here are some examples.

> "[Depth] You could have easily decided to go with a different person for the job, but you didn't, [Gratitude] and so I want to thank you for giving me this opportunity."

> "[Depth] You could have easily kept this frustration to yourself, but you didn't, [Gratitude] and so I want to thank you for sharing this with me so I can make things right."

> "[Depth] You could have easily stayed home and stuck with what was comfortable, but you didn't, [Gratitude] and so I want to thank you for being here today."

A Commitment to Action

At some point, we've all experienced an awkward silence. In the case of creating Depth, that awkward silence is like a windshield that begins to fog up, and without a commitment to corrective action, you lose the clarity that you had before.

So how do we show a commitment to action? We script out step one. By sharing what you can do immediately, you are showing the other party that you are choosing action over information. Information seekers might say something to the tune of, "Thank you for bringing that to my attention. I'm going to think about what you've said." To the customer sharing a concern, this feels like a slightly more elegant way of avoiding the issue. An apology finishing this way is a future apology waiting to happen. Jay Baer, author of *Hug Your Haters*, shared that "Customer service has become a spectator sport, and your online panel of judges can award or deduct points for speed, execution, and style." So what can we do instead? We can commit to taking action, matching the effort they've made to provide feedback, and following in kind. Remember, showing gratitude for feedback is professional, but taking no action is a breach of service.

Here are some examples:

> "[Depth] You could have easily decided to go with a different person for the job, but you didn't, [Gratitude] and so I want to thank you for giving me this opportunity. [Action] If you're open to it, then I'd love to get started right away."

> "[Depth] You could have easily kept this frustration to yourself, but you didn't, [Gratitude] and so I want to thank your sharing this with me so I can make things right. [Action] If it's okay by you, I'd love to give you this lesson on the house."

> "[Depth] You could have easily stayed home and stuck with what was comfortable, but you didn't, [Gratitude] and so I want to thank you for being here today. [Action] My mission is to show you a great return on that investment within the first fifteen minutes of your appointment."

Sometimes it takes a challenging situation, something that may rock you to your customer service core, to find the need to create depth. More often than not, whether it's at work or at home, communication breakdowns can usually be traced back to one party staying on the surface, failing to recognize the depth of the issue. Not anymore. Remember, every tough conversation has an alternative that would leave you without a willing partner in communication, so treat feedback as a gift, because they could have easily kept it to themselves.

CREATING ALTITUDE

We have a saying at work: "Dance problems are always plural, but their dance journey is unique and singular." Creating altitude helps people appreciate the singular qualities of their decision to use your product, frequent your business, or take your advice. Their Backstory, the challenges they've faced, or the moments in their lives that led them to you make up their customer fingerprint. Unfortunately, in the service industry, we can easily look past their singular journey and lump them into the bulk aggregate of every other customer. But we don't have to, and it all starts with losers in the Olympics.

Zoom Out to Zoom In

After years of training, excruciating effort, and personal sacrifice, you've made the Olympic diving team. The event is life changing and the competition is staggering, but you manage to block that all out and execute the dives you've been practicing for what seems like forever. When it comes time for the scoring, you sit, soaking up the moment while soaking in the post-dive hot tub. No medal this time, but plenty of memories and a bright future moving forward. So, here's the question: Did you really lose?

There are the internal wins, like the feeling of being a part of something bigger than yourself and proving to yourself that you're capable of greatness. But one thing we're forgetting is contrast. Imagine now if your Olympic swim coach came to check in on you after the scores were announced and said, "You may have placed seventh here at the games, but that also means that you placed seventh in the world, not just against the eight people in your event. You represented our country, and that means that you beat out millions of people, whether you faced them in competition or not."

It's easy for the competitor to zoom in and focus on the bad feelings that come with a defeat, but a great coach understands that perspective is the key to appreciation. By zooming out to the entire country, the eight people expand to millions. This creates a positive perspective when the coach zooms back in on the achievement, even if it was seventh out of eight competitors.

So how can we apply this to a customer service environment? Let's imagine a personal trainer with a client who shows up every morning at 6:00 a.m. for her appointments. The trainer could greet her each morning, run her through the different exercises he has lined up, and congratulate her on reaching fitness milestones, but how would that differ from any of the other clients he has? Instead, what if he recognized what makes his client's path unique?

"Sarah, how many people do you think are still sleeping right now instead of pushing themselves to improve like you are?" he says.

"Gosh, probably millions, when you put it that way," she says.

Then the trainer zooms in. "Exactly! Just think, you are knocking out your goals before millions of people have even rolled out of bed. I wish I had more clients with your level of dedication."

Three Zoom-Out Options

Zooming out starts by shifting the focus from the individual and widening the lens to a larger group of people. This can help you to create a "plural problem and singular journey" type of response. It keeps the professional in a positive, process-oriented frame of mind without it coming across as insincere.

Here are three areas to use as zoom-out segments:

1. Last Known Destination: Compare their most recent environment to their current one to help create contrast and positive perspective.
2. The Law of Averages: What is the common approach or problem that they can identify with?

3. People They Know: Sometimes it's not what you know, it's who they know.

Last Known Destination

Let's say that your customer arrived for their lesson after slugging it out in bumper-to-bumper traffic from work. Instead of jumping right into the content of your lesson, you could ask, "Mrs. Customer, out of everyone zoning out in bumper-to-bumper traffic, how many of them do you think are stopping on their way home to have an appointment like this to relieve stress?" This approach works with any last known environment. Whether that's coming from a busy day at work, school, or changing diapers, the professional that points them out is earning points with his clients.

Here are some examples for someone showing up a little late to their personal training appointment:

> Average Personal Trainer: "Hey Joe. Glad you could make it," the trainer says with the slightest measure of sarcasm, making Joe wonder if it would have been better if he'd just called and canceled.

> Service-Driven Personal Trainer: "Hey Joe. Glad you could make it. Listen, out of everyone that was out there in traffic with you, how many of them are investing in themselves like you are right now?"

Joe takes a minute to let the thought sink in. "Probably no one," he says.

The trainer's face brightens, "Exactly! You're taking the lead. Now let's get to work."

For every sarcastic "nice of you to show up," there's a cancellation in an average professional's future. Using the Last Known Destination puts the professional in a position to mine for empathy. Here's another example that I'm hoping everyone has a chance to experience.

Have you ever flown to Hawaii? The allure of the beautiful vacation spot can often lose its Mai Tai luster once you hop on a long flight with nothing but the Pacific Ocean as your scenery for what can seem like forever. But the people of Hawaii, particularly those in the tourism industry, are masters at empathy and have the Last Known Destination choreography down to a science.

Upon arriving at your hotel, you're greeted with a smile, a lei, a tropical beverage, and a "Welcome to Hawaii." This combination is in direct contrast to your Last Known Destination—whether that was the freezing weather of your hometown, the long flight over, or airport customs. The greeting is an instant reminder that you are now, officially, on vacation.

A final example comes from my personal life, mixed with my professional life. "I understand." "I see you." "I get it." These are all welcome phrases of empathy that can be expressed both verbally and nonverbally. As a parent, we can be both the seekers and the signalers of these messages within the parenting community. If a kid is having a minor meltdown at the mall, I'll send my parenting signal of "I get it," with a nod and a smile.

When my daughter, after many successful flights before the age of three, decided to cry nonstop on our way home from Disneyland (it was an hour flight that felt like nine), it was the knowing glances from other parents and reassurance from a woman behind us that got us through it.

"I know how hard that is, and you guys are doing great," she said.

Maybe it was the physical fatigue, or the emotional exhaustion, but her words hit the empathy bullseye. There was a definite catch in my throat when I thanked her.

Let's explore how this can work in an area of your business that you will likely run into more than, say, coaching new parents through traveling challenges with their toddlers—a different kind of support. In this case, it's the type you give by phone or chat.

If acknowledging the issue of wait times is par for the course, then failing to do so would be a definite bogey. Here's how you get an eagle: empathy and appreciation.

Example:

Average Service: "I want to apologize for the long wait time."

Customer Service Pro: "I apologize for the long wait time. You could have easily given up, but you didn't, so thank you for sticking around."

Average Service: "Sorry, we've been really busy today. How can I help you?"

Customer Service Pro: "Thank you for being so patient. I'm going to make sure that we solve this problem so you can get back to enjoying our product the way it was meant to be."

In both examples, what do you notice about the Service Pro? They're speaking to the feeling, showing empathy and appreciation, and this puts their customer's effort on a pedestal. We'll call that altitude. Experts in skydiving and customer service understand that, without altitude, any decision to jump could be fraught with peril. So, communicate your altitude to your customers before you try to solve their problems, so that jump isn't more dangerous than necessary.

The Law of Averages

Think back to that glorious time in your social development known as your teenage years and you'll find plenty of problems that are common but felt shockingly unique when they happened to you. Whether that was anxiety about your first day of high school, the awkwardness of dating, or a big pimple on your forehead, those situations may have felt exclusive, but they were all average teenage problems, not just yours.

The same can, and should, be said for your customers. When anyone is venturing in new territory, the law of averages isn't readily available to the consumer. It is, however, available to the professional, and that perspective can be vital data.

Let's say your client is having a difficult time sorting through the fine print on a new investment opportunity. You could make them feel even more like an amateur by saying, "I don't see what the problem is. Can you hurry up and sign or we'll miss this opportunity?"

Instead, after seeing their frustration or fielding their concern, you could respond with, "Do you know who else had this exact same problem?" Insert a little pause for dramatic effect. "Everyone." At this point, if this is in person or through a video conference, you should see some visual confirmation of concern being released from their body. "Everyone runs into that same issue, but that's why I'm here. Let me help make sense of it all so you can have some peace of mind with this opportunity."

The phrase "adding insult to injury" doesn't always mean physical harm or a verbal tongue lashing. When we are outside of our comfort zone, we have injured comfort. The insult is when that risk leads to embarrassment, and your shield of persistence gives way and your ego is exposed.

But all of this changes when you have a guide, armed with the vital intel that is the Law of Averages. Is there a time in the process of what you do where average people run into trouble? Share it. Is there a turning point that most people reach that can unlock more appreciation for your product? Share it.

If any of this conjures up The Secret Mission from earlier in the book, then you're well on your way to mastering your Customer Service Choreography.

People They Know

Knowledge can be both a blessing and a curse. Having the details on how to properly execute a stuntman-quality 180-degree parallel parking job might cause you to be a little less patient if you worked weekends as a driving instructor. Author John Maxwell said it best: "People don't care how much you know until they know how much you care."

We're going to take that one step further: it's not what you know, it's who they know.

"Out of everyone you'll see on Monday, how many could say that they learned how to drive a stick shift over the weekend?" Notice that this had nothing to do with the expertise of the professional. Instead, you can demonstrate expertise in the ability to show how much you care about the client.

Other times, you can make the query a little more specific to help create an appreciation for their venture into the brave new world that you're guiding them through: "Out of all of your married friends, how many do you think spent this much time and effort on their first dance like the two of you are?"

Finally, we'll consider the people they know as a way to gauge the support system they may or may not have and to help you refine your strategy: "Out of all of your friends and family, who would have the most dramatic response when you show up in this new suit?"

This may prompt responses that range from something that sounds like the fun banter of a celebrity talk show to something that requires more care, attention, and empowerment for your client.

In my case, I had a student who, when asked this question, responded quickly in a sharp whisper: "No one." The kind woman who had been so animated describing her love of golf and her longtime interest in dancing seemed to shut down, like a spy who suspected that the room contained listening devices.

This sent up an alert to the customer service detective desk in my mind, and so I continued down that trail to get a better idea of what I was dealing with. As it turns out, in her culture, a married woman dancing with another man, who wasn't her husband, was taboo. Her husband had no desire to dance whatsoever, despite the fact that it had been a lifelong passion of hers. So she decided to make the bold step and pursue something, despite all the danger it presented to her life. It was that important.

That made it important to me. Here's an example where one simple question can reveal a greater truth to work from. A truth that has less to do with your expertise with your product and more to do with your expertise with connecting to people.

CHAPTER 9

The Way You Make Me Feel

In dancing, or customer service, the goal of your choreography is to deliver more than just a sequence of rehearsed patterns; it's to make someone feel something. We've explored the fundamentals of things like The Backstory and Muscle Memory, we've aligned those into conversational frames like "the sooner, the sooner," and now it's time to present these skills with feeling. Or, more specifically, with the right feeling.

Imagine, for a second, that you walked into work, following your normal routine, only to find one significant adjustment waiting for you: German supermodel and megastar Heidi Klum is standing there, following you with her eyes, and not saying a word. She's holding a clipboard, looks at it, marks something, then looks back at you. Can you imagine the feeling?

With your curiosity piqued, along with your adrenaline, you might look around for hidden cameras or blurt out her name, but all the while, Heidi continues to study you, checking things off on her clipboard and not offering any explanation whatsoever.

In this scenario, what would you assume she was evaluating? Would you take a mental inventory of your outfit and curse yourself for not wearing your best "power outfit?" Would there be details, like hair, makeup, or a failed exercise goal that would immediately, upon German supermodel inspection, take on much more significance?

Most importantly, would you assume that Heidi was forming a positive or negative opinion of you?

With all things being considered—and with zero context whatsoever—it would be safe to say that this encounter, as novel as it might be, would be equal parts bizarre and unnerving. Just based on who she is and the role she plays professionally, it would be far easier to assume she was picking apart your fashion choice than, say, picking you as her new best friend.

Now let's consider an alternate version of our story. This time, when you arrive to work, Heidi meets your gaze, smiles, and approaches saying, "I'm so glad you've made it. My name is Heidi Klum, and you've been nominated by your coworkers to receive a fashion makeover."

The nerves of impending doom would be replaced by exhilaration. Sure, your heart would beat just as fast, but not because of a threat to your fashion safety. That two-car garage in your brain with spots for both nervousness and excitement would choose excitement (it's a convertible, by the way).

While this certainly sounds like the opening to so many before-and-after shows, if we peel back the reality television layers, what we can find is a skill that is both essential and easily overlooked: being disarming.

Being disarming is the ability to reduce the tension in a conversational setting, whether it's through reassurance, well-timed humor, or giving a little context with a smile.

In the first version (let's call it "Silent Heidi"), it was the opposite of disarming. Had that situation really occurred in your workplace, the shock and excitement of being in the same room with a celebrity would have imploded under the weight of her awkward silence. Even if it had been a non-supermodel, the absence of a greeting (combined with the appearance of a silent evaluation) would have a similar "arming" effect.

There's an old phrase that says that "silence is agreement." Without a disarming voice, the only voice you can listen to is the one in your head telling you that there's a threat. The silence on the other end will confirm that feeling of "I don't belong here," even if it isn't true, resulting in a socially awkward snowball effect that will pick up more confirming negative evidence, usually ending in a discontinued experience. Think of how men might feel when they are in a shop like Victoria's Secret, or in my case, it's the wide-eyed "please help me" look of someone walking into their first dance lesson. Every business has a version of this feeling, regardless of industry. The effects will only last as long as it takes for a disarming professional to replace the awkward feeling.

Which brings us to scenario two (let's call it "Makeover Show Heidi"). Notice that this greeting was immediate. Whether it was part of the script or just Heidi's awareness of how intimidating it could be for non-supermodels to see her in person, the immediate outreach, paired with down-to-earth context, is critical. Even though the makeover would involve an evaluation, having that stated in advance would create something more exciting than threatening, thus disarming the situation.

On the job, we can all be Heidi Klums. As the professional, you possess more power than you might realize. Whether it's your expertise, the price point of your product, the product itself, or the lack of familiarity with your business, these can all add that silent, protective statement of "you don't belong here." By initiating a warm greeting, you're doing more than just verbalizing page one of your training handbook. You're transforming your business from something that makes your client feel like they're trespassing to something that feels inviting.

Want to be a little more disarming? Want to feel more like the customer service professional you want to be? Let's explore some quick and easy ways to make Disarming a part of your Customer Service Choreography.

1. A Genuine Greeting: How do you normally greet a customer or client?
2. Add Context: What are the details that could easily go unspoken that will probably put your client at ease?
3. Use "Connecting Humor": You don't need to be a stand-up comedian to lighten the mood; you just need to be observant.

A GENUINE GREETING

Not to get too philosophical, but why do you greet your clients the way that you do? Is it the way that you'd like to greet them or the way you've been told to? We've all been to a theme park where the attendant mumbles the phrase "enjoy your ride" over the PA system with about as much enthusiasm as you'd have changing a diaper. Maybe saying "enjoy your ride" is on page one of the training manual—or maybe somewhere in the history of that theme park, a socially savvy employee decided to say it with a smile and people loved it. They loved it so much that other employees tried it, managers took notice, and it was included in the training program, leading to what we have today: a poor recreation of something that started out as sincere, like a game of telephone where the original message gets lost in translation.

So, what's the solution? You can audit your greeting. This doesn't need to be revolutionary, but it can simply start with the question: How are we trying to make our customers feel, and does this greeting deliver that?

At the dance studio, we deal with people who range from wanting to try something new, like salsa lessons, to those that have severe anxiety of stepping onto a dance floor. So, if our standard greeting was "Who's ready to start dancing?" it would be met with mixed reviews. Instead, we approach our new students with an equal measure of enthusiasm to meet them and support to help them get started.

"Welcome to Arthur Murray. It's great to meet you. Today's lesson is going to be easy, and you'll be dancing within the first five minutes. Are you ready to get started?" This works like a warm blanket in cold weather and helps even the most timid to let their nerves melt away.

One of my favorite examples of this comes from one of our senior teachers, Evan. From a distance, it might look like he's playing out a scene from the *Wizard of Oz* where the characters prepare to embark down the yellow brick road. Upon closer inspection, it's a master class in being Disarming. When teaching a couple, he walks them across the carpet right up to the edge of the dance floor and says, "I want to tell you both something: Today is a celebration. Once we cross over this threshold, you'll never have to say you don't know how to dance anymore. Are you ready?"

You can probably surmise that he's an excellent teacher, and that's before he's even taught a single dance step. He understands how to reduce nerves, instill confidence, and turn something as simple as stepping onto a dance floor into a milestone moment.

ADD CONTEXT

I was very fortunate to be a part of the Arthur Murray International training team. For the half dozen of us, our duties were to be the designated trainers for our worldwide organization. We worked tirelessly on our content, delivery, and responsibility as ambassadors of our brand. One of our training weekends (more like a boot camp for keynote speakers) was held at our company headquarters in Coral Gables, Florida. After some very nerve-racking exercises on eliminating filler words—which included a small audience of our peers holding clickers they'd use whenever they heard an "um"—the president of our company popped his head in.

Immediately, everyone sat up a little straighter. He listened for a minute to one of my colleagues, nodded in agreement, and then looked down the conference table directly at me.

"Christopher," he said in his smooth Australian accent, "I need to see you as soon as you are all finished." I could feel my face heating up, my heart sank to the floor—I must have looked like a new driver being pulled over for the first time.

"Uh, okay," I muttered. My colleagues didn't make things any easier. As soon as the door closed, there was a pause, then half a dozen faces turned in my direction, and said, "Oooh, someone's in trouble."

I held my hands up in as a gesture of my innocence, but the ribbing continued—that is, until the door opened back up. It was the president. My mind cycled through all the possibilities of what my crime could be, but he looked at me, then at the group, and said, "Don't worry, you're not in trouble."

When he left, what followed could best be described as a coordinated and simultaneous sigh of relief. My friends patted me on the shoulder; some looked at me like I had just dodged a bullet. It turns out that the president just had a question about something to do with our website.

What's the point of all this? Context.

Context should solve for the following questions:

> "Did I make the right decision?"
> "Do I belong here?"
> "Does this professional enjoy working here?"

When someone is operating on your turf, you are the keeper of context. You can use that context as a temporary platform to create a barrier, or you can share that context to establish a connection. In the dance world, this can happen when a professional seems to care more about their own dance ability than their ability to teach people to dance. You might see this type of character dramatized in reality dance shows or movies; checking on their student is always secondary to checking themselves in the mirror.

"Do I belong here?" is the first question on the minds of every potential client. While our intended and obvious answer is "of course they do," we could be steering our customers away from feeling welcome without even realizing it.

Shop Talk/Industry Jargon

Using fancy industry talk or overly technical explanations may keep someone feeling more knowledgeable in front of their client, but it doesn't give the client an affirmative to that original question, "Do I belong here?" Feeling confused, on top of attempting something new or different, isn't a great recipe for future success.

To avoid this, your role is to demystify the experience. This can be done by replacing industry talk with easy-to-understand phrases. If the microprocessor industry is about reducing the size and time to transfer information, why can't we do the same thing with the way we speak? The technology of communication needs to be updated regularly, scanned for connection errors, and streamlined to the most easily consumable size.

Here are some ways to relay the vital information without creating unnecessary distance with your client.

1. "All this means is…"
    If you've got something technical that needs to be conveyed, and you don't want their eyes to glaze over, you can say, "We're going to use the open API key to improve the workflow. All this means is, to make this work, we're going to superglue these two programs together." Whether you're talking about exhaust manifolds or mortgage paperwork, the phrase "all this means is…" is the piece of choreography that helps break apart technical information into the right-sized service portions.

2. "All we're going to do is…"
    Are you teaching something? Does your service involve a process? Whether you work in technical support, help Disney guests construct their own lightsabers, or teach someone to ride a bike, your role as a service professional is to break down a teaching process into easy steps. Providing a deluge of information will overwhelm the client: "Billy, I need you to balance yourself, but that can

only happen if you have enough forward momentum, which is why you need to apply more pressure through your quadriceps muscles. I don't care if you're six years old, this is how you ride a bike, or bicycle, if we want to be more accurate." Instead of all those steps, it's better to provide just the next one: "Billy, all we're going to do is pump your legs. I'll be right next to you."

"All we're going to do" forces you, the professional, to consistently scale down each step. Want a master-level example of this? Take a look at a LEGO instruction manual. As daunting as the build may seem, sometimes the manual will dedicate an entire page just for a single brick being added. This reduces the size of each step and builds in moments where the builder can feel some success. The byproduct is a sense of accomplishment (and hopefully something you won't step on later).

3. "And we call that…"
    We refer to this bit of choreography as "The Physical Before the Label." We'd rather have someone try something out physically before we hit them with the technical term for what they're doing. The label can be a barrier to entry, like dancing the tango, for instance. Most non-dancers assume that you need to have grown up in South America and have the flexibility of a ballerina and the ponytail of Antonio Banderas to execute the dance. So, instead of telling our students, "Now we're going to do the tango," we'll say, "All we're going to do is three walking steps and one side step." Then, after a few tries, we'll do the big reveal: "And we call that the tango."

In the Orson Scott Card classic *Ender's Game*, Ender is a young boy who believes the video simulation he's using is a training program for protecting the world from extinction. Later, it's revealed that the simulation is actually the real thing. Why all the cloak and dagger? Because if we've never danced the tango, or saved the world, it would be hard for our minds not to stand in the way and block us from seeing what is possible.

The "label" can be anything. Whether it's a medical procedure or the actual label of a garment you're selling, it holds enough power to repel people if it isn't used correctly. You'd rather try on the Gucci dress before being reminded that it's a Gucci by a less-than-helpful sales associate. If the label of every muscle was described in detail before you had to work out, you'd lose motivation. In writing, the common phrase is "show, don't tell" and the same can be said for customer service. "And we call that" is our gateway to a big reveal, to let our customer have an experience first before the details.

USE "CONNECTING HUMOR"

If the skill of being disarming were art, humor would be considered one of the great masters. Nothing can lighten the mood and jostle things back to normal faster than a good laugh. Connecting humor is a term I use that keeps the Backstory and bigger picture of your client in mind, rather than a joke that isn't relevant to the situation—and definitely never a joke at your customer's expense.

Connecting Humor became my standard icebreaker whenever I'd meet new students. I'd check their names on my clipboard, smile, and say, "Mr. and Mrs. Jones?" They'd confirm I had the right people, and then I'd introduce myself: "My name is Chris, I'm going to be your dance teacher, and I just want to apologize. It's my first day on the job and I'm extremely nervous." I'd say this last part with mock seriousness, followed by a grin. Sometimes, they'd laugh right away, or other times they might have a puzzled look and I'd reply, "I'm just kidding, but it is my first day on the job with the two of you as students. I can't wait to show you how easy this is going to be."

It was simple, just enough to make a quick connection, and it helped build momentum from the onset. Why? Because it's always safe to assume that a new customer is a little nervous. Had this been a joke about three blind nuns walking into a bar, the odds would, most certainly, not have been in my favor.

Connecting Humor should never come at the expense of a colleague or another client. I made this mistake with a good-natured teacher who would often assist with my Wednesday night classes. I saw the class as my own version of *The Tonight Show*, but my cohost was the target for a lot of my humor. Looking back, I traded some funny moments for my professionalism, and I could have made some better choices. Don't get me wrong; the humor was not inappropriate on the surface, but it was a missed opportunity. I used humor as a tool to build myself up, instead of to collaborate and build her up as well. Just because someone laughs doesn't mean that they really found your joke funny.

Connecting Humor is Honest

If you make a mistake as a professional, the survival mechanisms in your brain will campaign for you to cover it up at all costs. But this is a missed opportunity to show your client that you are, in fact, a human. It's also a great way to use some humor to reduce the tension enough to make a connection.

At some point in your restaurant life, you've probably seen a tray of food meet an untimely end, complete with shattered glass and maybe even a few feelings in the process. In the midst of the chaos, and apparently part of a weird custom that probably originated at summer camp, the diners in the restaurant will usually clap, whoop, and cheer. While most waitstaff would probably prefer to sweep themselves into a corner along with the debris, those that smile, wave, or laugh off the applause demonstrate a sense of humanity and humor. The situation may not be ideal, but the response certainly is. Can you imagine the alternative? The tray, the shattering of glass, and then a stoic reaction as if it never happened?

So, if you blow it on a call, let your customer know. If you forget the keys to the home you're showing, be honest about it, laugh it off, and you'll be a grade-A disarming service professional. Even when things don't go quite as planned, that's your opportunity to show your client that you're a human, but with the confidence to have a laugh at your own mistakes.

Connecting Humor Gone Wrong

It's one thing to laugh at a mistake, it's another thing to call your competence into question. I made this mistake. It was the first time I'd ever been reprimanded by my boss, but it was rooted in an attempt at humor. My Newcomer group classes were a big hit and so my franchisee, Patty, informed me that I was going to be bumped up to the big leagues: the Advanced Class. She wanted to help establish my credibility as a teacher with the high-level students, many of them having started before I was employed. I was Patty's assistant in the class; she tossed me as many opportunities as she could to demonstrate my dancing and teaching ability, but I decided to bat them all away.

"Now I'm going to have Chris demonstrate this cha-cha pattern, so you can see what we're working on," Patty said.

Then I followed, like someone who flunks the improv assignment in drama class, "Actually, if you want to see what it really looks like, you should probably watch Patty. Her hip motion is much better than mine," I said with a laugh. This was just the beginning, but Patty, being the consummate professional, picked up where I'd left off, laughed at each of the self-deprecating comments, and we got through the class. From a humor standpoint alone, I felt like it was a home run. But when Patty brought me into her office, I realized quickly that it was just a series of fouls.

"Don't ever do that again," she said. Her voice was shaky, like she was trying not to scream; I'd never seen her that way. I couldn't form any response; I just cycled through the mental footage of what she could have been referring to. "I've spent weeks building you up to the advanced students, telling them what a great dancer and teacher you are, and all you did was make fun of yourself," she said. The truth came crashing down like a tray of drinks, but there was no applause. It was awkward and embarrassing. I could feel my face getting hot and somewhere in the back of my mind, a negative voice said, *You're going to get fired.* Patty continued, "Do you understand? By making fun of yourself, you were also making me look bad in the process." Another crash. My face could have melted ice, and I realized full well why she was so frustrated.

After a series of apologies, she reminded me of the bigger picture: "Those students may think you're funny, but I want them to see what a great teacher you are." What I didn't realize until that moment was that self-deprecating humor was my crutch, a preemptive strike at criticism (you may think I'm bad, and I'm going to say it first so I'm in control) and it was slowing down my growth as a professional.

Imposter syndrome may have the strongest grip at the beginning of a new job, but it also has long tendrils that can reach anytime you're attempting something new. Connecting humor must never come at the cost of your professional reputation. Leveraging a laugh for your credibility is a long-term loss for a short-term gain. Not to mention, that choice would be customizing the customer experience around the professional instead of the client; servicing based on our feelings instead of the customer's.

CREATING A WELCOMING ENVIRONMENT

So, we're greeting people with a genuine interest in their story. We're avoiding shop talk, reducing the barriers, and using humor to feel more human. Now what? To turn this idea into a real initiative, and the initiative into a movement, you'll need to take this from the individual level and scale it out to the entire tribe. Here's how.

Positive Gossip

We all know the power of standard gossip. It's like a whirlwind that can build in its intensity and transform into something on the Fujita scale in terms of total damage. But what if you could create the opposite? Like a tornado that rolls through town, installing swimming pools and adding new landscaping, positive gossip can have the same type of effect.

Think of the transformative power of a brand-new haircut. For some reason, it creates enough positive change that even the most critical people can find an excuse to check themselves a few extra times in the mirror. Then, adding to the glory of that experience, someone sends a compliment your way. Your inner voice approves the message, you smile, and thank them for the kind words. This is a standard compliment.

Now imagine the feeling when you hear someone complimenting you to someone else. Whether it's a haircut, the quality of your last presentation at work, even the craftsmanship you employ with a breakfast burrito, it doesn't matter; a compliment *about* you feels more magnified than a compliment said directly *to* you. That is positive gossip. Here are three ideas for how to create it in your business.

1. Share a Common Backstory

We know what a vital role Backstory plays in our Customer Service Choreography to our clients, but now, through Positive Gossip, it will be about our clients. For example:

"Do you see that woman walking in right now? Her name is Mathilda, and her story reminds me so much of yours. She is such an inspiration, and I think you're going to love meeting her."

By sharing a common Backstory, I've created a connection before I've even made any introductions. In doing so, I've transitioned one anonymous person into a potential connection. Note how The Backstory continues even in the introduction.

"Hi Mathilda, I wanted you to meet Jane. She got started with her personal training with a similar story as yours—she's a mom, and she wanted to invest in her own personal development—and since you've been such an inspiration with what you've shared about your experience, I thought you'd be the perfect person for her to meet."

It's natural to see other people as threats when you're in a new environment. Positive gossip, with a shared Backstory, can eliminate that completely.

2. Establish Credibility and Reassurance

Think of how often a frontline employee may pass the baton of responsibility up the hierarchy to a coworker or manager. Now imagine how often that employee takes the time to build that person's credibility or reassures the customer in the process. This version of positive gossip is designed to do just that.

"What I'd love to do is have you chat with Alex. Not only is he one of our senior managers, but he's also the perfect person to solve this situation, and I'm certain he'll do that for us."

Compare this with "Let me go ask my boss." Who the person is far outweighs what role they play, and by establishing their credibility and reassuring the client, you can turn a typically awkward exchange into something meaningful. As with the last scenario, the positive gossip continues with the introduction.

"Hi, Alex, this is Ernie and Sue. They're interested in that new promotion and I was mentioning to them that you're the perfect person to talk to. If you have a minute, could you assist us with that?"

My wife Daisey loves this topic. She sees credibility and reassurance as two different ends of a bridge. One without the other is like a bridge with only one side. If the reassurance is there but credibility is weak, it's like a rope-and-timber bridge you might find in an Indiana Jones movie. To make a bridge, or connection, between two people, you've got to build both parts with equal commitment.

FINAL THOUGHT

Dance moves without technique are like song lyrics without the right pitch; you need to work both halves of the equation to unlock the solution. When it comes to our Customer Service Choreography, we can't just rely on a few clever things to say. We need to solve for the mood that we set and the environment that we create, and we do that by being disarming. Without it, even the overwhelming beauty of a German supermodel can't keep your high-touch service from sounding off key.

CHAPTER 10

Putting It into Action

We've come to the point in our Customer Service Choreography where you can take what you've learned from simply good information to a game-changing shift in your business. It all comes down to application, to practice, to keep digging. My favorite story, the one that kept me pushing when times were most daunting as a business owner, comes from *Think and Grow Rich*, the seminal work by Napoleon Hill.

He shares the true story of a man named R. U. Darby. (Honestly, I'm not sure if that's an alias, or a tongue-in-cheek challenge to anyone reading his story: "Are you Darby?") Darby staked a claim during the gold rush out west.

> After weeks of labor, he was rewarded by the discovery of the shining ore. He needed machinery to bring the ore to the surface. Quietly, he covered up the mine, retraced his footsteps to his home in Williamsburg, Maryland, told his relatives and a few neighbors of the "strike." They

got together money for the needed machinery, had it shipped…Darby went back to work the mine.

The first car of ore was mined, and shipped to a smelter. The returns proved they had one of the richest mines in Colorado! A few more cars of that ore would clear the debts. Then would come the big killing in profits…Then something happened! The vein of gold ore disappeared! They had come to the end of the rainbow, and the pot of gold was no longer there! They drilled on, desperately trying to pick up the vein again—all to no avail.

Finally, they decided to QUIT. They sold the machinery to a junk man for a few hundred dollars, and took the train back home. Some "junk" men are dumb, but not this one! He called in a mining engineer to look at the mine and do a little calculating. The engineer advised that the project had failed, because the owners were not familiar with "fault lines." His calculations showed that the vein would be found JUST THREE FEET FROM WHERE THE DARBYS HAD STOPPED DRILLING! That is exactly where it was found!

The "Junk" man took millions of dollars in ore from the mine, because he knew enough to seek expert counsel before giving up.

If you had been there, knowing what you know, what would you have said to Darby? "I know it's tough…I know you can't see it yet…but you just have to keep digging." In all the work I've done with business owners, there were plenty of ways I was able to help upgrade the tools they were using, but it usually came down to a story similar to Darby's. They stopped digging too early.

Hopefully, you're on the verge of an extraordinary breakthrough when it comes to high-touch service. And, from this book, I hope you've learned the moves and assembled the tools to help. We just have three feet of earth to move, to push past barriers with the promise of something better on the other side. Here's where we take our tools and begin to see how well they dig.

HERE ARE SEVEN PRACTICE PRINCIPLES FOR IMPLEMENTING YOUR SERVICE CHOREOGRAPHY

1. Change Is Not Practice

It was the night before our first professional performance, and I was panicking. It wasn't that I was afraid to perform; it's that I was worried it wasn't going to be fancy enough. So, my solution was to completely dismantle our cha-cha choreography. Daisey, bless her heart, went along with it, but when we performed it less than twelve hours later, not surprisingly, it was an absolute train wreck.

What I learned, the hard way, was that my heart was in the right place—I wanted to make our dancing better—but my tactics were the problem. I focused on what we were dancing instead of how we were dancing it. Had we run through our original routine emphasizing some critical, measurable ingredients like posture, timing, or styling, we could have saved ourselves a lot of heartache.

Let's apply this same cautionary tale to the practice of your Service Choreography. Your first instinct when rehearsing this material might be to change it, but that won't change the skill or the results in your organization.

2. Avoid the Curse of Information

Remember, when information goes up, application goes down. You'd never make any progress if you decided to "research" the best exercises to hit your goal weight. As comical as that may sound as a strategy, it is a sound strategy for those struck with the Curse of Information.

Information, and the process of searching for it, can feel productive enough as an exercise that we lose sight of the ultimate goal of applying it in our day-to-day activity. If you were wrongly convicted of a crime, a lawyer researching every last detail of your case probably wouldn't cause any alarm. But if that same lawyer didn't show up for your trial, only to tell you later that he was still busy researching, he would probably be out of a job.

Doing more research, taking things under consideration, and seeking out new and better ways to perfect things are all part of the vicious trap of the Curse of Information. Perfectionism is just a fancy version of procrastination and any action that doesn't lead to implementing is a potential information curse you should audit.

3. Stretch, Sprint, then Sculpt

Our daily staff training improved dramatically when we scripted out a regular schedule of events. It took us a few years, and plenty of frustration, to do the same thing with our competitive dance practices. Once we set up a scripted agenda, we understood the expectations and could create a sense of urgency to achieving them.

It's no different than a great workout. You'll usually start with some type of stretch to prepare your body for the upcoming work, then you'll shift into some cardio to get your heart rate up. Finally, you'll lift weights and home in on the specific muscles you're targeting. Let's take the same approach with implementing your service training.

Stretch: If stretching is a preview of an upcoming workout, the same can be said for your service training. In this case, you're going to set the scene for you or your team: "In this next scenario, your client's current schedule won't get them the results they need in time for their event. Let's use The Negative and Muscle Memory to improve their appointment frequency."

The goal is to take the problem, assign a solution, and set a clear objective before you begin.

Sprint: Let's say you manage a group of two dozen people. Rather than having them each apply the training one at a time, the goal is to give everyone as many reps as possible to get their implementation heart rates up. You can do this by having everyone pair up and attempt the objective.

Set a time limit and, just like a great personal trainer, be clear about how many reps you'll do before switching things up. "Hi, everyone, we're each going to do this scenario twice. This will give everyone a chance to get the nerves out and get some repetition under our belts."

Your approach during the Sprint is to clear out all cobwebs of nervous energy and unfamiliarity. Just like a workout, the sprint stage has one goal: to get your heart rate up through exertion. From a workout standpoint, this helps you break a sweat, feels productive, and prepares you to receive the next stage. In business training, the same is true. You may not break a sweat physically, but if your heart beats faster from the effort you're exerting, you're one step closer to being able to execute the skill when the client is in front of you.

Sculpt: It's so much easier to criticize than it is to coach. During the sculpting stage, your goal is to coach around the most objective details. Similar to the gym, you can only attack one training machine at a time. Here are some examples you can layer in:

- Content: If you've outlined the three major bullet points of the presentation, have the person on the receiving end pinpoint whether each was mentioned or not. How clear was the message?
- Timing: If you began the rehearsal with a ninety-second time limit, could you execute the same presentation in sixty seconds?

Interestingly enough, reducing the amount of time has a dramatic effect on the clarity and urgency of a recommendation.

• Power-Ups: Whether it's swapping out a bland word for a superior one or adjusting the order of the presentation, pick a single power-up to improve the scenario.

Once you've finished a circuit, repeat as necessary. Remember, a single, measurable improvement is much better than several negligible ones.

4. Wrong Way Is the Right Way

We learned the importance of being disarming in the last chapter. Imagine what could happen if we disarmed an entire training exercise. One of the best decisions we ever made in training our team was adding an exercise titled "Wrong Way/Right Way." It's simple: Start with an objective (see number three), and your goal is to have one person create the worst-case rendition of that scenario.

This does far more than get laughs; it sets the floor for the skill. By establishing the zero end of the spectrum, you create a reference point for the peak end of where the skill can go. Not to mention, your service team has a secret, sadistic longing to experience the feeling of completely botching a service interaction.

Opening with the wrong, then correcting those wrongs in the second rendition, gives the listener a chance to pinpoint the specific improvements. These should be fairly obvious, but it creates an opportunity for both the listener and the speaker to stay primed toward the differences from the bad version to the good.

5. Find the Assassin

Let's consider an active combat zone for a second. For the record, this is not a euphemism for the break room in your business. If you consider the element of surprise as a key factor in military success, where would you rank these two combat components: a tank and an assassin? In terms of stealth, it's an easy choice. The tank can be heard from half a mile away. It's the armored equivalent of a bull in a China shop: blasting and rolling unapologetically down the warpath. Conversely, the assassin is whisper-quiet. There's no armor to speak of and no bulky weapons. The assassin's entire body is his weapon, and stealthy movement is his primary military advantage.

When it comes to service, there are mistakes that are big, loud, and painfully obvious, like a tank. There are others, however, that are much harder to spot, like an assassin. If a tank problem is a zero on the scale of subtlety, an assassin may score in the nine or ten range. From a training standpoint, this exercise is designed to improve the awareness of the minor, missing details that can feel right to the professional but produce the wrong result.

Here's how it works: Give the speaker a specific objective and a specific missing ingredient. For example, they could have all the right content but poor body language, or they could have a great tone of voice but poor content delivery. Keeping the problem a secret turns the listener into an active "ninja hunter" (for lack of a better explanation). Their goal is to listen to the presentation and pinpoint what the subtle, assassin-level problem was.

You can try varying the problems, then have a discussion about how easy it is to commit these stealthy errors and why fixing them can have a big impact moving forward.

6. What's Different?

Hopefully by this point, your band of assassin problem hunters are highly tuned in the ways of customer service training. Let's take it up another notch. If self-discovery is essential to driving a sense of ownership, consider this exercise your key.

Your training scenario will begin with a basic objective like "Greet this new client when they walk in." The professional will execute the basic task and the listener will play the role of the client.

Next, you'll separate and give the professional a specific upgrade: "This time, instead of staying behind the desk, greet them from farther away and then walk over to meet them in the lobby."

Repeat the scenario but inform the listener that there may be an upgrade of some sort and their job is to pinpoint it, being as specific as possible. At the end of the second go-round, you'll ask the listener to share what was better from version one to version two. They may nail the improvement right away or they may be in the ballpark, but anything that speaks to the secret improvement you suggested provides a sense of ownership for the listener who spotted it and validity to the professional who adopted the feedback.

7. The Weighted Mock: Creating Smarter Simulated Clients

Up until this point, those playing the role of a client are essentially a human version of a video game NPC (non-playable character). At this stage, we're going to alter things a bit and give the client more of a voice to pressure test the professionals. (Note: This stage should only be activated once your team has trained through the earlier stages).

In this scenario, you're going to plant an idea with anyone playing the client, and that idea will have some sort of trigger. We're not talking about a complex system like the Rube Goldberg machine to open the gate in the movie *Goonies*, but think of this as some kind of action and reaction if something in the professional's delivery misses the mark. Using a simple scoring system (ten being completely connected, open and trusting; one being the opposite), the professional may say something that reduces the client's original score, and they will exhibit some type of physical or conversational clue to show that.

For example, "In this first round, you're going to play the role of the brand-new golf student. You're nervous and self-conscious, so let's say that you're already coming in at a four. If, at any point, Mark uses terminology that sounds technical, you're going to drop down a point. If Mark uses more connecting terms and encouragement, you'll go up a point. When he asks to schedule your next appointment, if you're under a five, you'll avoid scheduling anything."

From there you'll give Mark his objective: "You're going to give your brand-new golf student a quick lesson. At the end, you're going to recommend a program and schedule their next appointment."

As you can see, this could be more like a trap door than a Rube Goldberg, but hopefully you get the idea. Our real-life clients are much smarter, and more responsive, than video game NPCs. Creating this action-and-reaction variable to the training scenario allows everyone to bring, or develop, their customer service A game.

At the dance studio, this began with a spur-of-the-moment idea to help curb a problem that our team didn't see as one. After all, they were consistently one of the top five locations in the world, had plenty of recognition in our company, and many of our individual teachers had won some prestigious awards. Translation: They knew what to say, but their results were beginning to taper off. I was able to identify the problem, the assassin lurking in camouflage, which was something completely inconspicuous: shoes.

For context, our dance students are like fitness clients—they see an exponential return on their investment when they keep their appointments closer together. Our team understood that, believed in it, and could recite training we had covered on the topic. One area we commonly focused on was arranging a back-to-back appointment for ninety minutes, rather than just sticking with a forty-five-minute lesson. But we began to see a drop-off in the activity in some of our students regardless.

I decided to use the Weighted Mock. I had half of my team play the role of teachers, and the other half play the role of students. I explained to everyone playing the role of teacher that their goal was to wrap up their lesson on the dance floor and then invite their students to stick around for another appointment spot that had just opened up. An extra lesson builds faster muscle memory, there's less review time, and it creates a faster breakthrough for the student.

What I told the professionals acting as the students was something completely different. "The moment they step off the dance floor, the chance of you staying for an extra lesson is going to drop down by two points. If they sit down to chat with you, it will drop some more. When that happens, start taking off your dance shoes and putting on your regular ones, just like our students do. The moment you take your shoes off, there is zero chance that you will stay for the extra lesson."

We ran the simulation, and one by one, they each had settled into a comfortable procedure of walking off the floor, sitting down, taking notes, and then asking for the extra appointment. Not only that, it was after they had taken their dance shoes off. One by one, each person playing a student would smile, shake their head, and decline the invitation I had asked the teachers to rehearse. This seemed to scramble their circuitry.

The teachers looked perplexed, to say the least. I asked them what they felt like the issue was. Some said it was the content of the lesson, others emphasized the wording of their invitation, but not one of them picked up that the shoes were the death knell to their invitation.

We tried it again with the adjustments that they suggested and they ran into the same results. So I huddled the teachers up and explained, "The further you move from the dance floor, the less likely they're going to say yes."

We tried the scenario again, and the teachers started to say things like, "I'd hate for us to lose all the momentum of this lesson," and "Let's build on what we've done right now so we can unlock your muscle memory." And sure enough, one by one, the students started to leave their shoes on.

THE TAKEAWAY

Training exercises are great. They can create a simulated amount of pressure that can resemble the real thing. But if you've ever sung your heart out in the shower only to turn away a chance at singing karaoke, you understand that everything changes when your skill is taken to a live audience. If the previous exercises helped to sharpen our tools, what will follow next will get you as close to breaking ground as a book can take you.

- 100 percent of the fear (only some of the time): If you were asked to make ten phone calls, how would you rate your fear of rejection, failure, or cold calling on call number one? For all intents and outbound call purposes, the highest amount of fear would occur on the first phone call. After all, you're stepping into the unknown, and even if you're armed with the best Customer Service choreography, you're relaying it to a live audience.

But what happens to that same fear by the second or third call? Based on familiarity alone, there's no way that someone could feel the same high-intensity fear that you might on call number one. I'd go as far as saying that the fear would reduce anywhere from ten to twenty percent from one call to the next. This would reduce the fear to less than half by the fifth call, and it could be virtually nonexistent by the final few.

When fear is no longer an issue, you're like a singer whose microphone finally starts working. You're speaking with your true voice.

When we first took ownership of Arthur Murray Hayward, Daisey and I had no advertising budget. We were operating with a prepaid ad in the Yellow Pages and our current student body. So, I decided to make phone calls to former students. As I searched through the records, I found a treasure trove of student files that dated back to the 1970s. My sole mission was to share the news that Arthur Murray Hayward was under new ownership, that we wanted all of the previous students to see what the new environment was like, and we'd love to invite them in for a free lesson to see for themselves.

There were a lot of phone calls.

So many, in fact, that there wasn't a response that could dissuade me from making another call. I believed, down to the core of my being, that anyone who came into this new studio environment would get a far better experience than the one that had caused them to leave. In some cases, I had the wrong number; in others, they'd say, "That's my father's name, and he passed away about ten years ago."

So I'd reply, "He still has a free lesson on his account, and we'd honor that for any next of kin too." Every file was a glimpse into our company's past and an exercise on how to beat the fear of application.

By that point, my fear was nonexistent. I was speaking with my full voice and with enough conviction and enthusiasm that we had some wonderful students, from a few different decades in our studio's history, return to take lessons with us. Looking back, that was a time that Sun Tzu would refer to as "the death ground," a point where an army is backed into a corner, retreat is not an option, and their only means of survival is to fight. Based on our business assets and general liquidity, it's safe to say we were on the death ground. Had we not been, there's a very good chance that those calls could have been made at a leisurely, comfort-based pace...or not at all.

But those dusty cards (I can still smell them) taught me that a steady onslaught of application will beat back the stifling effects of fear. Think of the fear or anxiety of applying new training as mildew: It prefers a dark place. It wants to be left alone, preferably in a damp recess, so it can grow, take residence, and consume the space with its retch-inducing presence. Each time you encounter new training and apply it in earnest, you're putting that fear into a bright, dry space. When you operate with momentum, high repetition, and with a goal of trying it ten times without abandoning the task, you're fighting the mildew of fear.

Whether this is brought on by your own "death ground" scenario, like bringing a business back from the brink of disaster, or just by sheer determination, there's no version of you that is better off with fear as your coworker.

So, make ten calls. Withhold any opinion until you've completed all ten. By that point, you'll be operating in that fearless zone—call it a flow state, the natural-use stage, or too tired to care—and you might find that the next ten calls, or interactions, are a little easier.

LEAN INTO THE CHALLENGE OR CARRY AROUND REGRET

For years, I dragged my feet, moaned and groaned, and did everything I could to exude my displeasure at practicing our competitive dancing in the morning. Through the beginning of my career, I was a professional night person, expert sleeper, and perennial procrastinator. That is, until I started dancing with Daisey. She was the opposite of all those things. She loved her morning routine, had a can-do attitude, and detested the idea of putting something off if it could be done immediately. For the record, she hasn't changed in that regard. What I didn't realize until an unfortunate amount of time later was that I was trying anything to avoid the work, even if I agreed that it would make us better. I understood it but didn't want to lean into it.

The penalty for that was a lot of wasted time and, much worse, a lot of regret. If R. U. Darby was really a question and not a name, I certainly was a Darby. Instead of digging that remaining three feet to gold, I rolled my eyes, made more coffee, or put in a lackluster effort. My behavior was a tank, at times, and an assassin at others. I had the tools, a willing partner, and all the motivation to receive the reward at the other side, but it was the digging—the extra effort required—that threw me off.

It was far easier to blame others for our results (like my partner for asking me to practice in the morning or my body for not looking like someone else's), but that just kept me in the same spot.

John G. Miller's book *QBQ!* was like a stick of dynamite for me. Learning to take accountability revealed that on the other side of my own three feet of earth wasn't a trophy or prestigious competition result. It was a new and improved version of me: the partner that Daisey deserved all along, the guy that saw that every practice was an opportunity instead of an obligation and that feedback wasn't a threat but just another way to get better.

Fortunately, with the right amount of digging, you can reach a place where you can exchange regret for solid gold lessons. The kinds of things you'll treasure, polish, and share with anyone who will listen. The kinds of lessons that will refine your purpose and give you the confidence to do the same.

Think of how many bizarre twists and turns led you to this moment in your career. Think of how many close calls you might have had while driving or decisions that you look back on and realize were loaded with things best described as "the butterfly effect." Every challenge that could have defeated you, didn't. You're, quite literally, undefeated—even on Mondays and even if you don't always feel that way. This is the depth behind your personal Backstory. Every decision you make to challenge yourself to dig that extra three feet will be a tribute to all those moments that could have stopped you but didn't. Your Backstory is your leverage to move the challenges in front of you.

EPILOGUE

Sometimes your motivation to do something is a placeholder for something so much greater. In my case, I began my career at Arthur Murray first as an attempt to impress a girl and second as an attempt to prove that same girl wrong when she said that I'd never be any good at the job. In short, I began my career motivated by hurt feelings, a desire for retribution, and a chip on my shoulder. Little did I know that a chance encounter would reveal just how silly that all was.

I was on my way to work on a sunny spring day in 2002. By that point, I was a senior teacher with an apartment not far from work. I had a great girlfriend who happened to be my dance partner, the school I worked at was one of the top Arthur Murray locations in the world, and I was making enough money that my family was excited for my career path. This was the kind of day where kids in San Jose might decide to hit the beach instead of school, but not me.

I hopped in my 1968 Mustang, a car I still own today, and drove with the windows down to take in the mix of fresh air and old-car smell. Listening to the one and only tape I kept as the permanent soundtrack of my vehicle, *Francis Albert Sinatra & Antônio Carlos Jobim*, was the final ingredient to my pre-work routine that could best be described as driving revelry, bossa nova edition.

As I was heading down Lawrence Expressway in Santa Clara, my sunny drive came to an abrupt halt. Over the sounds of Sinatra and Jobim came several honks. Not the light honks you might hear if you left your blinker on or were taking too long to merge onto the expressway. These were the kinds of honks where the horn might change key from overuse, the horn-honk equivalent of all caps. It startled me, to say the least. I looked all over, like a swarm of bees had entered my vehicle, and then, to my right, I saw a face and my heart sank.

In the lane to my right, matching my fifty-miles-per-hour speed, was Scarlet. The girl who had told me so coldly that I would never make it as a dance teacher was right there, smiling and waving at me. "How are you doing?" she screamed from one lane over.

"Doing good!" I screamed back. I hadn't seen her since that fateful day. Years had passed and my life had certainly changed, but seeing her still brought back the sting of those words. But none of that seemed to affect her at all. She asked me where I was going, and when I said I was going to work, thinking that might end our conversation in a convenient goodbye, I was stunned when she said she would follow me there. Deep down, I knew I could tell her off, share the truth, tell her she was wrong and feel some strange satisfaction, but part of me felt like I should just let things play out, and so she followed me to work.

We arrived a few minutes later to the back parking lot in the strip mall that contains Arthur Murray San Jose. For all she knew, I worked at the Burger King or Home Depot next door. We both got out of our cars and did some surface-level catching up. I didn't mention anything about my teaching job. It just didn't feel right, and I was beginning to realize how much I had changed since I'd been that guy, devastated by her outlook on my proposed career path.

When the conversation had reached a natural lull, I told her, "It was great catching up. I've got to get into work now."

Then, a flash of comprehension seemed to light up her face and she said, "Wow, I'd love to come check out what you do." At that point, my ego took the reins, and I led her there. Without saying a thing, I walked her right through the front door of the dance studio.

It was the same doorway I had been too scared to enter for my first interview, and all of a sudden, the girl that made me second-guess my capability to walk through that doorway was cautiously trailing behind me. I turned to her and told her to come on in. She looked like she was being invited into a tax audit, the pace of her steps dropping to a tentative half speed. As I looked ahead to the receptionist desk, I thought to myself, *This can't be happening.* On the wall behind the desk were awards from our most recent convention, including a top teacher award for yours truly. I turned my back to the wall and faced her like someone finally spilling a carefully guarded surprise: "So, yeah, I ended up getting that job at Arthur Murray." My ego-focused desire to delight in this news took a backseat when I noticed how rattled she was.

She forced a smile and seemed to make a shift of her own to one of authority: "That's great. I was thinking of maybe looking into some advanced shag or Balboa classes. Do you guys have anyone here that can teach that?"

Then, placing the cherry on top of the sundae of this bizarre, one-in-a-million encounter, my coworker, Monique, appeared after picking up the tail end of the question and said, "Oh you're talking to the wrong guy," she said with a witty smile. "He's only the swing king around here."

I shrugged my shoulders, did my best to convey as much sincerity as possible, and said, "It really was great to see you." Then, there were some expected pleasantries exchanged on the way out. But seeing her that day closed the loop on that cycle in my career path. It also revealed something to me that I had yet to truly realize: that chance encounter would have made for the perfect ending to my time at Arthur Murray.

But that motivation had such a limited lifespan. That Backstory was enough to get me through the door of my interview, but it was no longer the fuel I was using to move further in my career. Those feelings were all replaced, right out from under my nose. Michelangelo, one of the artistic masters in all of history, once said, "I saw the angel in the marble and carved until I set him free." My motivation felt similar. My initial feelings of spite, embarrassment, and vindication were replaced by the stories of my students and the progress I was fortunate to be a part of. I witnessed so many angels being freed from the stone of nerves, insecurity, and a lack of confidence.

The smile on my face when I went to work was to continue that work. To ask the questions, make the connections, and carefully chisel away any doubt and defensiveness they may have had. But actually, my students seemed to also have chisels of their own. It seemed like in every lesson I taught, I was equal parts student and teacher. In that bizarre moment, I learned that the hurt young man I had been, absorbed only in personal feelings, would never have lasted to the point I was at. I realized that the camaraderie and mentorship I had received made me just as much an advocate for the Arthur Murray organization as a consumer as our students.

Over the next five years, there were some major milestones, from saying goodbye to my colleagues at Arthur Murray San Jose to becoming business partners with Daisey in Arthur Murray Hayward, getting married in 2005, having our son in 2009, and saying goodbye to our competitive dance careers later that year. We've had peaks and valleys as we've hired staff, trained managers, had more kids, developed new business owners, opened more schools, and had more kids, but there's one important thing that stayed constant through everything.

A heart for service should never be restricted to your time at work. If you've done the work—chiseled away the worry, the familiar, and all the debris of marble that encapsulated what you are truly capable of—then let the rest of the world see that angel fly. Ask your family questions, find the Backstory of how your parents met or how they overcame a tough challenge. Share a Secret Mission with your kids when you take the scenic route on your next family road trip. Explain to a friend how much potential you see for them, do it with the conviction of someone just three feet from gold, and use The Negative to help them steer clear of a path that could cause regret later.

I hope that this Customer Service Choreography has helped you to see how impactful you can truly become, regardless of your position, and that you can make a difference that goes beyond a transaction or an online review. If you're willing to dig, to make recommendations from the heart, and to invite your customers to achieve more, you can do something that will truly change someone's life—and, as an added bonus, your life just might change for the better in the process.

ACKNOWLEDGMENTS

Thank you to all of the supporters of this book. Especially those that did so when it was still just the seed of an idea. Your belief is what brought it to this point.

Dawn Smart
Alexis Morales
Joey & Madison Sena
Joe & Leisa Howard
Brandon & Kristen Perpich
Mike & Suze DeSante
Quinton & Theresa MacAdam
Hunter & Maria Johnson
Nate & Rachel Martin
Tiffany & Andrew Higgins
Justin McClendon
Rodney & Gisella Schultz
James & Jessica Dutton
Taras & Wendy Denysenko
Augusto & Brigita Schiavo
Emily Bergman

CJ & Jenny Gomez
Lania & Mike Berger
Lisa MacLaggan
Richard & Marianne Myers
Russ Clark

Bobby, Mark, Patty, Christina, Juan, Cari, Monique, and Federico - A great team combined with great times = wonderful memories.

To my staff, family, and friends, thank you for listening to my stories, counting my analogies, and encouraging me to continue.

And to all of my students, you have all been extraordinary teachers in my life. Thank you.